PEACE TOGETHER

PEACE TOGETHER

The Courageous Story of an Army Nurse and a Medic
Who Went to Vietnam So That Others May Live

Terah K. Hensley

Copyright @ 2021 Terah K. Hensley

All rights reserved. No part of this publication may be reproduced or transmitted in any form or by any electronic or mechanical means including photo copying, recording, or any information storage and retrieval system now known or to be invented, without permission in writing from the publisher or the author.

Name: Terah K. Hensley
Title: Peace Together: The Courageous Story of an Army Nurse and a Medic Who Went to Vietnam So That Others May Live
By Terah K. Hensley
ISBN: 978-1-953114-44-0
LCCN: 2021923818

Subjects: 1. History/Military/Vietnam War
2. Biography & Autobiography/Military
3. Biography & Autobiography/Medical

Cover photo: Justin Gallo
Author photo credits: Heath Hensley
Photo credits: Michael & Shirley Hensley; personal album; used by permission, 2021.

Published by EA Books Publishing, a division of Living Parables of Central Florida, Inc. a 501c3
EABooksPublishing.com

For Lieutenant Shirley Harbers, for Mike the medic, and for all those who went to war so that others may live.

FOREWORD

"You wanna do what?"

This was our response to our daughter-in-law's request to write a book about our story. The story of where and how we met is unique and unusual but never did we consider it to be book worthy. Terah Kay can be persuasive and persistent, so we didn't expect her request to go away. The prospect of mining those memories of our time together in Viet Nam was intimidating and we knew the process would be humbling, challenging, and perhaps painful. We eventually said yes. At the very least, our grandchildren would have a written reference to how their Nana and Papa began a life long relationship. But more importantly, we realized that our small story was part of a much larger one. Although now almost forgotten, the Viet Nam war impacted our entire generation at the time.

The war entered our homes every evening on television. Everyone knew someone serving in Southeast Asia. Political justifications and explanations of the war became a source of great controversy sparking demonstrations and riots across our nation. It was an unpopular war, killing a lot of people.

As young Army recruits, we don't recall being asked our personal or political preference for a war assignment. We just went. Amid protests and political upheaval, it was our patriotic privilege to answer the call of our Country and serve as a force for freedom in Viet Nam. What ever personal reservations we had were neutralized by our desire to serve others who would need our medical abilities. It was truly an honor to stand with so many who gave so much for that cause. America is a great land of the free because of the selfless sacrifices of the brave.

We had to provide our author with memories so she could tell our story with words. This required us to mentally transport ourselves back in time and recall details from our year together in Viet Nam. In doing so, we experienced two extremes. We remembered the quiet tranquility of sitting on the edge of a rocky cliff, looking out over the South China Sea, watching the morning sun break the horizon, and sharing our hopes and dreams for a future in the world beyond that sunrise. We also remembered the screams coming from blood soaked stretchers of young American soldiers crying in pain, pleading for help, and begging for life. Then the silence following their final breath.

Ours is a story of those two extremes and everything in between.

Whatever public notice or attention comes from this story, it is our prayer that the focus would not be on us. But rather on those who didn't have the chance to live their lives, to pursue their dreams, to raise a family, spoil their grandchildren, or to grow old with their soulmate. Those true heroes that didn't come home ...

Michael Hensley

INTRODUCTION

Meet Mike and Shirley. They are an interesting pair of people who God undoubtedly created for one another. I am their daughter-in-law and from the moment I decided to be a writer, I knew they were to be my first subjects (or victims, as I'm sure my father-in-law views it, but only half jokingly). Growing up as a part of their family since I was thirteen years old, I had heard bits and pieces of their story over the years and knew there was something incredible to be unearthed and shared with the world.

You see, Mike and Shirley are old now. Their wrinkles and their gray hair, the beautiful signs of weathered souls. These people you're going to read about, they have survived. They have known real hatred. They have fought to be forgivers, they have loved without condition. They have lived. Their story is like none other I've ever known and to be the one who gets to share it with you, dear reader, is a great blessing on my life. I'm so excited for you to meet them on these pages!

I feel like it's important to note, before you get started, that Mike and Shirley did not want to tell me their story. They are incredibly humble people who thought their lives weren't worth words on a page. They didn't think of themselves as book-subject material, they didn't view their pasts as heroic or think that they deserved any more highlighting or attention than anyone else.

Permission to dig around in their mental archives and record their history, took some serious convincing. They had to take a huge, uncomfortable step toward trusting me, based on my word that they could. That I would devote all of my energy, emotions, and talent to receiving their painful pasts with the proper weight and handle the telling of their story with the utmost care. I promised I would protect their memories, that I would portray the truth on these pages and that I would present their history in a way that honors and respects their experiences.

Over a five-year period, we traveled back through their pasts with countless interviews. We combed through old photo albums, enjoyed old home movies, and read old letters. We looked up newspaper articles, watched documentaries, and we even traveled to Vietnam for their return to the only place where their suffering could be fully reconciled.

Mike and Shirley and I wanted to write this story for our family, to preserve an important piece of Hensley history. We also wanted to tell it so that we could add to the slim collection of first hand accounts from the Vietnam War, to preserve a piece of World History. But most importantly, we wanted to write this story for the thousands of medically trained service men and women of the United States Armed Forces, specifically, those who served in Vietnam.

We believe that these brave souls have a unique perspective of the war. Each soldier had different, important duties, and that led to different experiences of the war—and all their stories deserve our time and attention. Our focus here, though, is on the medical side of the war. The viewpoint of the nurses, medics, and doctors has scarcely been told, and that is its own tragedy. Our hope is that this book will, at least, humbly add to Vietnam War history, and at best, bring healing to those who have shared in these experiences.

Thank you for taking the time to get to know Mike and Shirley. I can assure you this, reading their story will be challenging, joyful, and worth every minute you spend with them. Writing it, changed my life.

-T.K. Hensley

Contents

Dedication i
Foreward ii
Introduction v
1. War Bound 1
2. Good Morning, Vietnam! 24
3. It Don't Mean Nothin' 40
4. A Warm Welcome 76
5. China Beach 93
6. Forbidden, Hidden Love 118
7. We Gotta Get Out of this Place 157
8. Short Timers 194
9. Peace, Love, and Freedom! 218
10. Back to the World 233
11. Country Bound 243
12. Mission Accomplished 252
Epilogue 265
Thanks 269
Bibliography 274
About the Author 276

Chapter One

WAR BOUND

Shirley Jean H. came into the world on April 18, 1948, in the small town of Montgomery, Ohio, just outside of Cincinnati. The third of five children, Shirley was the one who spent the most time around her father, Marion. She would hand her dad tools in the garage as he worked on his cars, and help him cut the grass in the yard. Wherever he was, she was right by his side. A daddy's girl right from the start.

When baby number five came onto the scene many years later, Shirley's mother Mary was 41 years old, and baby Janet was born with Downs Syndrome. Shirley remembers the adults referring to her sister as a "blue baby", a term used when an infant is born with a blue complexion due to lack of oxygen in the blood. Almost immediately there were complications and changes to the family dynamics when they brought Janet home. Shirley was 12 years old and understood from the beginning that Jan was different from the rest of them. Nevertheless, she loved taking care of her baby sister, carrying her all around the house, helping her mom feed and play with sweet little Jan.

Marion struggled to come to grips with the fact that he had a child who was different and who would need lifelong parental care. He grew quite discontent with his situation and over time, he began to resent Mary. He thought that if Mary hadn't chosen to have a child in her forties, they would have all been healthy kids and his life could've been happy. He did not ask for a divorce, but he didn't want to have another child like Janet and so he kept his distance from Mary. She was a devout Catholic and it was against the rules to prevent pregnancy in any way. For Marion, it meant he would no longer be intimate with his wife for fear of another unhealthy pregnancy.

Mary wasn't sure what happened to their relationship. They never discussed the change, but she knew that it happened after Jan was born. Eventually, the distance he put between them became the new normal for their family and everyone seemed to accept it.

Unfortunately for Shirley, this is the same time that her father's attention became unhealthily focused on her. In his mind, his now unmet sexual desires, should still be fulfilled from within his own home. In the beginning, Shirley had no idea anything was out of the ordinary. She had only ever been a part of her family and figured that it must be how all families are. It must be normal. By the time she figured out that her father shouldn't be behaving the way he was with her, there was already a trajectory set, a routine, an expectation.

The more he abused Shirley in secret, the more angry and strict he became with her in front of the family. It seemed that she could never do anything right and was constantly being grounded for minor teenage offenses. If Shirley wasn't home for him to abuse, he took his anger out on the rest of the family, making it almost unbearable for them, to the point that Shirley felt guilty for being away from the house. She thought she could at least save the rest of her family members from him by staying home as much as possible. He allowed her to go to school, to keep up the appearance of normalcy, but that was it. School, home, school, home. Not a single other soul in the family knew this was happening to Shirley, and for a while, she wanted to keep it that way.

As she got into high school, she decided that she'd had enough. She was already living in her own prison, fighting with her dad on a daily basis. It was a hell that was eating away at her little by little each day. They'd have yelling battles, cursing at one another up and down the halls of that hopeless house and then she'd be forced to comply with his wishes just to have permission to leave. She finally decided that her best option was to escape. To run away and live with a friend. She had it all planned out. She was going to leave and never come back. She didn't know what would happen to the rest of the family, but she couldn't help them anymore. She was being ruined, broken, and utterly destroyed, every second she stayed there under his oppression.

Every time she would run away, the guilt would set in, that it was all her fault the rest of her family was now living in misery. She was seen as the troublemaker in the family, the problem child, and she knew that only she could make it better for everyone. Every time, she'd return home, deal with her punishments, and go back to the status quo. None of her friends ever knew the real reason why she was leaving home, she always told them that her dad was just too strict. She was comfortable with that explanation for their combative relationship, and as she got older, she became embarrassed to tell the truth. She wanted it kept hidden as much as her dad did. But the weight of carrying this dark and shameful secret was crushing her.

By the time Shirley started high school, she gained the courage and the knowledge she needed to do what was right, and she had started to tell all their secrets. First, she told her older brother, Jack, who immediately attempted to stand up to his dad. He confronted Marion and Shirley could hear them yelling back and forth. Unfortunately, Jack was just as intimidated by his father as the rest of the family, and nothing ever came of it. He was sorry he couldn't help her, and it tore him to pieces. He didn't know what else to do to help his sister and it caused him a great deal of anguish. Shirley was grateful Jack had tried to save her and she understood how much power her father wielded over all of them. She never blamed him for not being able to rescue her from their dad. Neither one of them knew how to tell their mom, knowing that it would break her heart, and they thought it was best not to tell their sisters either. The dark secret protecting Marion continued to be hidden from the rest of the family.

Shirley then told the priest at her church while in the confessional booth. Unfortunately, he never did a thing about it, which was shocking to Shirley at the time. She was sure the priest would save her. She later decided to tell a counselor at school, who promptly called home to ask her dad about the accusations. When Marion denied that any abuse was taking place, and told the counselor Shirley was a troubled child just acting out, the counselor apologized and never looked into it any further. Shirley got in big trouble at home and then later, at school, for lying. She learned pretty quickly that telling someone the truth wasn't going to save her. She was on her own. Help was not coming, rescue was not something she could hope for. So, she took matters into her own hands.

When she was a senior in high school, she was miraculously able to argue her dad into allowing her to go to the prom. If he didn't let her go, it might have been suspicious, and so with much reluctance, he gave his permission. She didn't have a date, with it being an all girls Catholic school, so she decided to ask the neighbor boy who lived across the street. Normally, she wouldn't be so brazen as to ask a boy she barely knew to go to prom, but it was all a part of her escape plan, and having a date was important. The neighbor boy was a shy kid, really sweet, and happily agreed to go to prom with her. Before they left, Marion gave him a stern look in the eyes and told him to have Shirley home no later than 12 o' clock.

When they got to the prom, Shirley found her best friend, Carol, to make sure the plan was still a go. She told Carol that she had permission from her dad to stay the night after prom if that was still alright. Carol said her parents were already planning on it! She felt bad for lying to her friend, but it was too risky at this point to tell anyone the truth, she just needed to get away. From Carol's house, Shirley was going to leave town. She didn't know where she was going to go, but the bus station wasn't far from their house, and in the morning, she'd be headed somewhere new. After a couple hours at the prom, Shirley told the neighbor boy to take her to Carol's house instead of home. The boy was hesitant, having received such a stern talk about being home by midnight from Shirley's father just hours ago. Shirley did her best to play it cool as she lied to him. She promised that she had just spoken with her dad on the phone, and he was okay with her spending the night at Carol's house. She felt bad for the sweet neighbor boy, that she used him to get to prom and to Carol's and he was going to have to answer to her dad later that night, but she figured he'd survive. She had to do what she had to do. If she was ever going to be rescued, she knew she'd have to do it herself.

By 5am, before Shirley was able to get out of the house, Marion had tracked her down. He was pounding on the front door, and when Carol's parents answered, he began screaming at them for allowing Shirley to stay the night without permission. When Shirley heard the commotion, she knew it was over. She didn't even try to explain it to Carol. She just silently accepted that she was never going to escape him and she walked out the front door without a word, also accepting her reputation around town as a troublesome youth.

Shirley spent the rest of her senior year at home, biding her time until graduation when she would actually be able to leave. She had applied and been accepted to attend nursing school and was looking forward to starting her new life, away from her dad, a life of freedom and maybe even happiness.

The nursing school wasn't very far from Shirley's house, so her dad allowed her to go without too much of a fight, as long as she promised to come home on the weekends. Shirley promised; she just needed him to pay for school and then she'd be free of him forever. She tried once or twice not coming home on the weekend, but when she called to check in, she'd hear about how awful life was getting for the rest of the family. If Shirley didn't come home, Marion punished everyone with his venomous mood, lashing out in anger. Shirley always heard about it from her mom and sisters and felt guilty enough to go home and make their misery stop. She was beginning to wonder if she'd ever be free from her father; it just seemed so hopeless.

One weekend, as the nurses were all planning to go out together, Shirley declined the invitation to join them, as she always did, but this time one of her teachers seemed to be more interested in Shirley's weekend affairs than usual. The teacher asked to speak with Shirley privately and wanted to know why she went home every weekend instead of going out with the other nursing students, making friends, and having fun. The teacher watched carefully as Shirley tried to sidestep giving an honest answer. She saw Shirley's eyes go dull and her demeanor change, she listened as Shirley's voice trembled ever so slightly with sadness as Shirley explained that her dad was very strict and would not like it if she didn't come home for the weekend. Shirley had learned by now that telling the truth didn't matter. No one was going to save her from her father, so why bother? But this teacher sat there looking at Shirley, taking it all in silently, and Shirley knew that her teacher knew. They stared at each other for a few moments before the teacher told Shirley to get in the car.

Shirley didn't argue, she got in the passenger seat of her teacher's car, hope rising in her chest. Could this be it? Could this be the day? Could she be the savior Shirley had been waiting for? They drove all the way to Shirley's home and when they came through the front door, her teacher looked her in the eye and told her to go pack her things, she would never be coming back. Shirley ran up the stairs as her father came to the foyer. Realizing what was happening, he began cursing at her teacher, calling her all kinds of names and yelling at her to get out of his house. Shirley heard her teacher yelling right back at him. She was telling him that Shirley was eighteen years old now and this was over. She would not ever be coming back to this house again.

Shirley grabbed her suitcase. Hearing the commotion below, she furiously packed what would fit—some of her favorite clothes and books, she threw it all in, desperately wanting to get out. She didn't have time to think. As the cursing and name calling escalated downstairs, she zipped her bag and hurried down the stairs, not making eye contact with anyone in the family, especially her dad. She ducked out of the house behind her teacher, into the car, and off they drove! Shirley sat silently in the passenger seat all the way back to nursing school, tears streaming down her cheeks the whole way. She was finally free.

At nursing school, she had become great friends with a girl named Barb, and Barb's family had become a second family for Shirley. They loved her to pieces and would send her food at school, and Christmas presents just as if she were one of their own children. It was wonderful to have them in her life, and she held onto those relationships tightly, thankful every day for Barb and her family.

A couple of weeks later, Shirley caught wind from a friend back home that in the local newspaper, Marion had legally disowned her. A legal disownment with a newspaper notice was a manipulative move meant to humiliate and ostracize her from the community she had grown up in; it was a public shaming. Shirley decided not to let it get to her. But it also meant that her father was no longer responsible for her financially. Her school bills were no longer his concern; her punishment for escaping his abuse. If she wasn't going to cooperate with his demands, he wasn't going to help her in life. She may have been his daughter, but he didn't seem to care about her future, what kind of job she may get one day, what skills she may learn, or what kind of adult she would become. He only thought of her in selfish ways, and if she wasn't serving his needs, he didn't care what happened to her.

After a meeting with one of the nuns at school to discuss why she wasn't going to go home to her family one weekend a month, as the school required, Shirley sat and listened as the woman called her dad and reamed him up and down about what a terrible father he was for disowning her in the paper and for being such a callous man. Shirley later found out from her mom that her father had become so upset at the nun during that phone call that he ripped the phone right out of the wall. Shirley was so glad she didn't have to deal with that kind of radical behavior anymore, and she hoped the rest of her family were okay.

Feeling like she had a new family to lean on, and being rid of her reputation as a troubled teen, Shirley started taking matters into her own hands once again. She didn't let her dad's withdrawal of finances get her down for too long. Instead, she got a job on the weekends working as a CNA (certified nursing assistant) at the local Good Samaritan Hospital. She decided she would put herself through school if that's what it was going to take. Plus, she liked getting the experience in the hospital, as she was still in nurse training at school. Her life was finally looking the way she wanted it to. She felt independent and for the first time since she could remember, she was excited about her future!

She started going to counseling to work through her past issues and to express her guilt for making it out of the house and living her new happy life, while the rest of her family lived on in misery. She told the counselor it was all her fault that the rest of them were being treated so poorly by her dad because he lashed out at them anytime she wasn't around. She knew she was never going back, that she couldn't, but she also knew she needed to get all these feelings off her chest if she was ever going to make it to that happy future she was dreaming about.

Every week, she went to counseling, and each time, she left a little lighter, both emotionally and physically. As Shirley felt more and more in control of her life and her future, she became a healthier person and the weight she had gained in her teenage years to ward off unwanted male attention, came melting off.

Shirley was making new friends in nursing school which gave her plenty of alternative places to go home to on the weekends with different girls from class. One of her favorite places to visit, besides Barb's family, was out to a beautiful piece of farmland where Bee's family lived.

Bee was another nursing friend Shirley made at school, and Bee's family loved to host Shirley for the weekends as well. They lived in a small, quaint town and Shirley thought it was absolutely gorgeous and perfectly peaceful! It was such a small town that when Bee came home from nursing school, with Shirley in tow, it made the local newspaper.

It was there that Shirley met a handsome young pilot named David. David was a few years older than Shirley, very confident and smart. He was good looking and successful and very interested in Shirley. They began dating right away and Shirley felt that her new life was shaping up quite nicely. She had a boyfriend, lots of friends, and was putting herself through school. She was free from the clutches of her father and her childhood, and would be spending her life working in a career that helped people.

David invited Shirley to come meet his parents and stay at their house some weekends when she would come to visit. They lived on a beautiful piece of property along the Ohio river, nestled into the side of the rolling hills. Across the road, there were cows grazing the pastures, and from their porch she could hear the cowbells ring. She absolutely loved it there.

Over time, as their relationship grew more serious, David couldn't wait for Shirley to drive up on the weekends, so he would fly his small plane to the local airport near the nursing school to pick her up. From there, they'd fly somewhere to spend a long weekend before he would drop her off again for school. Shirley thought it was like something out of a fairy tale, and her thoughts were all consumed by David.

One day, as David opened the door of his car for Shirley to get in, she noticed a child's car seat in the back. He told her it was for his nephew, and they went along without any more discussion about it. Soon after the car seat discovery, the phone calls stopped. He wasn't coming to pick her up at the airport anymore, and she wasn't invited to spend the weekends with his family. Shirley was devastated. She found out from Bee that he had started dating another woman from the town they lived in. Shirley was heartbroken by the sudden change in events. She had been literally sitting by the phone for hours and days just waiting for it to ring, waiting for him to call and he had already moved on without letting her know. She felt so used, and so naive.

She later found out that David had been married, had a child, and had recently been divorced. His ex-wife was from a different country and had taken their child back to her homeland to live permanently. All of this had been happening while Shirley was dating David, and she figured she must've been a needed distraction from his pain. It was a hard lesson and a depressing couple of months to recover from.

She felt bad for David, bad for herself, stupid for getting so emotionally attached, and all at the same time, she understood why he did it. Why he led her on, why he lied about the car seat and why he thought he needed to keep distracting himself with women. It was just so unfortunate that he wasn't mature enough to tell her the truth and to break things off with her like a gentleman instead of leaving her to figure it out on her own. She picked herself up, dusted herself off, and thought that the next time she decided to date someone, she would need to get to know him better before getting so attached.

WAR BOUND

Around this time, the Army recruiters came to visit the nursing school. They offered to pay for nursing school in its entirety if any of the girls signed up to serve four years in the Army Nurse Corp. In addition to covering the cost of school, they'd begin getting a paycheck as soon as they signed up as PFCs (Private First Class). It was perfect timing! Shirley had nothing to hold her back from traveling, had no future plans, and she thought it'd be a good way to meet more friends and see more of the world.

She also was the kind of person who loved structure in her life. The military sounded good to her. Organized and systematic, it had great appeal. She thought it was an easy decision. She wanted to be a nurse, and she could definitely use the money to pay for the rest of her schooling. She and Barb decided to sign up together. They were promised that if they signed on together, the Army would keep them together for their entire four years. Same training camps, same orders for service. They signed up right away.

After graduating from nursing school and becoming Registered Nurses (RN) they had to take their state board exams at the capitol, in Columbus. It took all summer to get their results back to know if they passed or not. Those who passed were immediately commissioned into the military as officers. She went straight from being a PFC upon enlisting while still in school, to an officer with her nursing degree. She and Barb were promoted to Second

Lieutenant and received their orders to report to Fort Sam Houston, a medical basic training camp in San Antonio, Texas. Shirley finally called home to let her family know that she was an officer in the Army Nurse Corp. and that she was moving to Texas.

At Fort Sam Houston, Shirley and the other nurses spent a couple of weeks learning all the ins and outs of basic military procedures. After firing their guns, learning the proper saluting protocols, and some rudimentary boot camp style training, they were ready to delve into their real work. Shirley found herself learning how to set up and operate M.A.S.H. units (Mobile Army Surgical Hospital) in the field. They replicated warlike scenarios and practiced functioning in wartime conditions. They provided on the scene emergency care to pretend injured men, all while the noises of war surrounded their tent. They spent three days running the portable emergency room, learning to care for injured men with little sleep, and with injuries they had not experienced in regular nursing school.

At one point, a man came into the tent with his arm blown off, and they asked Shirley what she was going to do about it. All of it was make-believe, but the pressure still seemed very real, and Shirley got to work caring for the man. It was fantastic, hands-on training for the women and helped them learn to focus on their tasks while many distractions threatened to break their concentration. None of them knew for sure if they'd be going to war, but the training was necessary for all.

Shirley decided after her experience at Fort Sam Houston that she actually wanted to go to Vietnam. The nurses had two choices as to where to report next. One was Fort Campbell, which meant they'd most likely be sent to Vietnam, and the other was Fort Bragg, where they'd continue military training and may or may not receive orders for Vietnam. She had enjoyed the M.A.S.H. training, triage, and emergency type nursing so much and thought she could make a big difference for the men over there fighting in the war, the ones who would really need a good nurse to potentially save their lives. No more pretending, no more scenarios, but actual life-saving work. She knew in her heart that she could do it, that she had what it would take to remain calm and focused, and she wanted to be there in the real aftermath of battle, where she believed she would be most useful. Shirley requested to be sent to Fort Campbell. Barb felt the same way and they agreed to volunteer for Vietnam together.

When they arrived at Fort Campbell, they joined together with another nurse named Pat, whom they had become close friends with at basic training. They all decided to get a house together off base. They would host gatherings and small parties together, playing games and meeting new friends. It was there that Shirley met a young medic named Darrell. He was extremely funny and seemed to always be able to make her laugh. He wasn't particularly handsome, but Shirley really enjoyed being around his positivity, and they soon began dating. It was very casual but was fun, and Shirley didn't take it too seriously. They'd hang out at parties, talk about what they were learning in training, and go on dates. It was just nice to have someone to do things with, but it wasn't love.

After just a couple of months, Pat received orders to report to Vietnam for one year. It was why they had all chosen to go to Fort Campbell, but it was scary at the same time to watch one of their friends get called to war. Over the next couple of weeks, Shirley really began to seek out time with Pat. There was something about Pat that she had admired since the day they met. Pat was different somehow. She was warm and kind, and seemed light in spirit. It was very attractive, and Shirley wondered what it was that made her this way. She thought that whatever Pat had, she wanted it too. She had observed Pat reading her Bible every morning, something Shirley had never been taught to do growing up as a Catholic. Pat seemed so enthralled with the Bible and would even talk about Jesus like he was her best friend. It was all so foreign and intriguing to Shirley.

One evening Shirley was walking past Pat's bedroom and peeked in to see her reading on her bed. Desperate for more conversation with Pat before she was gone, Shirley asked her what she was reading. Pat told her she was reading her Bible. Shirley knew there were people besides priests who read the Bible, but she had never met anyone like that, and she had never tried reading it herself. In fact, she didn't even own one. She asked Pat to tell her what it said, to tell her how she was able to understand it and why she was able to talk about Jesus the way she did.

Pat had been a Christian pretty much her whole life. Reading the Bible was a common daily routine to her. As she watched Shirley, standing there at her bedroom door, asking her to share what the Bible said, she could just tell that Shirley was reaching out, hungry for something more, thirsty to learn about the God she already believed in.

Pat and Shirley had a wonderful conversation where Pat explained that the Bible said Shirley could know God personally—that she didn't have to go through a priest to talk to God, that she could pray to him anytime she wanted and read his words on her own. She explained the significance of the person of Jesus and how he made a way for them to have direct communication with God and a forgiven path to Heaven.

When Pat was finished explaining all of this to Shirley, she asked her if she believed it all. Shirley said she did, and Pat took the opportunity to lead Shirley in prayer to become a born again Christian. To accept that Jesus paid the debt for all sins on the cross, making the way for a personal relationship with the Creator possible. Shirley had never felt more sure of anything in her life. In that moment, she knew it was all true, and she knew it was what made Pat different. From that day on, she wanted to read the Bible and learn about Jesus and God and be made new by truth. She felt hope rise again from within, a new hope that she would not be alone in her difficulties anymore, that whatever troubles may come, she would always have a savior and his name was Jesus.

Just a couple months after Pat left for Vietnam, Shirley received her new orders. One year in Vietnam. Barb received the same orders, and as promised, Shirley and Barb would be roommates stationed together in Nha'Trang. They would be leaving in just a few weeks' time.

Feeling the fear of being totally detached from the United States, Shirley and Darrell made a commitment to write to each other every day and to meet six months later in Hawaii, when she would have her R&R (rest and recuperation) in Honolulu. She didn't really want to be that serious with Darrell, but she also wanted to have someone to write home to, to tell about her experiences, and to hear about what was going on back home. A connection to the states that would give her a reason to get out her pen and paper and write to someone who would care what she was going through.

All through school and training, the recruits had seen and heard about the riots happening across the country. The young people, their peers, had been rising up in mass numbers to speak out against the war in Vietnam. The antiwar mentality was the culture of their youth. The music, the protests, the media, all reflected the sentiment that the country wanted their troops out of Vietnam. They didn't support the war, they didn't support the government, and they didn't support the military. Shirley stayed away from the protests as much as she could. There had been riots in her town and protesters marching against the continuation of the war.

Eventually, events like the Kent State massacre, where four students were killed by the Ohio National Guard while protesting the Vietnam War on campus, led to the polarization of the country. Many people hated the military, soldiers, and the United States government for its continued involvement and expansion of troops in the Vietnam War.

It was at this time, under this climate, that Shirley, Barb, and the other nurses became soldiers. The draft was in full effect, and as she watched young men ripped away from their lives against their will get hauled off to fight on some foreign land, she couldn't understand how the people blamed them for their involvement. It was a federal crime not to report for duty once drafted. Their only choice to avoid involvement was to desert their home country and become a national criminal, without the possibility of ever coming back home. Or, they could answer the call of their country, hope against odds to survive their year in 'Nam and come back home to live as free men.

She saw them come home, wounded and mangled, and then get spit upon by the men and women of their homeland. She thought it was shameful and she was glad that she was in the military. She wanted to help those young men to heal and recover. She wanted to do her part to nurse them back to life in a culture that hated them for doing their jobs. She knew she may be hated too for being associated with the war, but she didn't care. She was a nurse now, an Army nurse, and there were dying boys who needed her to show up for duty.

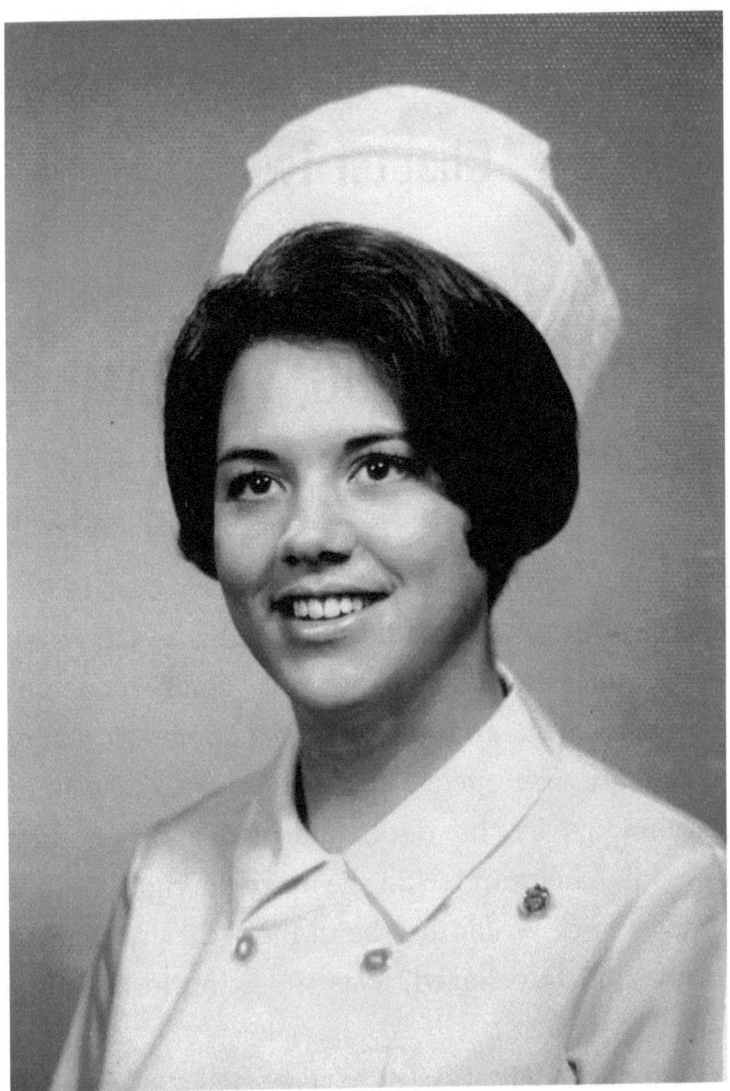

Shirley's graduation from nursing school.

Chapter Two

GOOD MORNING, VIETNAM!

Shirley arrived in Vietnam at the military base in Cam Ranh Bay during the middle of the night. As soon as she stepped off the plane, she was bombarded with unfamiliar smells, and she could hear bombs erupting in the distance. She opened her eyes wide to take in her surroundings in the dark, and floods of questions poured into her mind. Had she made the right choice in coming there? Would she be in more danger than she had previously believed? Was she going to be able to make it over there?

She thought of how she didn't know anyone around her and again, her ears perked up, recording new sounds as women rushed by speaking a language she had never heard before. Her heart raced and her throat tightened as she looked around, desperately searching to find a familiar face. Realizing she was on her own, she squeezed her eyes shut and hoped she would be with Barb soon. She told herself to stay calm, to just breathe deeply and say a prayer.

Forgetting her departure orders and ending up on a separate flight from Barb was quickly becoming one of her greatest regrets. She felt so lonely, knowing not a single other soul who'd stepped off that plane with her, and she started to feel sick to her stomach. Homesick for America. It was all so different from home, and fear crept into her young mind. With each new mortar round going off, her regret grew. As she stood in the dark taking all that was new, her mind landed on one final thought . . . What had she done?

She broke free from her daze, realizing that an officer was shouting over the noise and motioning for her to follow him. She obeyed the orders that she couldn't hear and went with him, desperately hoping she would be reunited with Barb right away. Instead, she was led straight to her barracks, which reeked of musty, damp canvas and tired, rotten wood. Again, she tried to say a comforting prayer and tried not to think about how anxious she felt. The cot was stiff and the wool blankets too warm for her Ohio blood. The monsoon outside slapped against the roof, like a great applause, welcoming her to Vietnam—welcoming her to the chaos and the brutality of the war, to the unfamiliar mountains and the unrelenting rain, and to her new home for the next 12 months. She spent the next few hours lying awake and staring at the ceiling, trying to figure out how to ignore the explosions and find some sleep. At some point, in the early morning hours, she must have finally drifted off. When she woke up, the sun arose, revealing the South China Sea.

After dressing out in her Army issued jungle fatigues, Lieutenant Shirley Harbers found herself walking up the ramp into an olive drab C-130. The bulky aircraft was headed north, for the US Army base in Nha'Trang. She found a seat among the black mesh nets hanging from either side of the plane and waited with anticipation. She couldn't wait to see Barb.

Her orders were to help the existing doctors and nurses effectively turn the Nha'Trang 8th Field hospital over to Vietnamese control. The Army would be vacating Nha'Trang in a short amount of time and needed to make sure that the Vietnamese could run the hospital on their own. Nha'Trang had seen a lot of action in earlier years of the war, but at this point, in May 1970, much of the conflict in that region of Vietnam was over. Shirley tried to imagine what her new responsibilities would involve as she helped the ARVN (The Army of the Republic of Vietnam) take charge of the hospital on their own. She busied her mind with speculations about her new job and tried to relax as the plane lifted off toward Nha'Trang.

GOOD MORNING, VIETNAM!

Barb and Shirley were finally reunited when Shirley was brought to their barracks upon landing. They embraced when they saw one another, and this helped to set Shirley's mind at ease, as much as was possible in wartime. She thanked God for giving her such a trusted friend. They were pleased to see that the Army had kept their word, and the two friends were able to become roommates in Vietnam. They became a great encouragement to one another, as they learned more about what their lives were going to be like for the next year.

Though the battles had slowed down in the area, the hospital was not without recovering patients. From time to time, it also still received badly injured soldiers who had so unfortunately found themselves standing on top of leftover landmines and booby traps. Bouncing Bettys were particularly popular among NVA (North Vietnamese Army) and VC (Viet Cong) soldiers who were charged with setting hidden explosives for the US boys to step on. These fierce little mines had a lightning fast trigger and upon being released by the foot of an American soldier, they would fly straight up in the air, between three to five feet high and explode right next to the vital organs of their victims. Packed full of scrap metals, they were very efficient at causing fatal wounds, especially if they made it to the chest height of the victim before detonating. The NVA and VC were very good at creating torturous ways to injure and kill the US boys in their jungle. Many of the traps were so brutal and feared that the Americans became religious in how careful they were to place their feet in each other's footsteps while humping through the bush.

They hiked with extraordinary care, when circumstances allowed them the time to do so, and kept a sharp eye out for anything even slightly out of the ordinary. Point Men had an extremely taxing job, being the first man in line to enter hostile and unsecured territories. They tried to do the seemingly impossible, which was to get their squad through enemy territory without detonating camouflaged booby traps, all the while looking out for ambushes. Running point was such a strenuous job that squads often rotated who would be tasked with the dangerous responsibility. Many such point men, as well as countless others, had found themselves standing in the wrong spot at the wrong time. However briefly their mistake had been, they had paid for it with their limbs, and oftentimes, their lives. This was the kind of thing that kept Shirley and her comrades working around the clock, even if the direct fighting in a particular area had decreased. Unfortunately, many Vietnamese nationals trying to live their lives during this time also found themselves stepping on hidden landmines, bouncing bettys, and booby traps. Shirley and her team treated tattered farmers, villagers, and children as well as the soldiers (Clark, 2002).

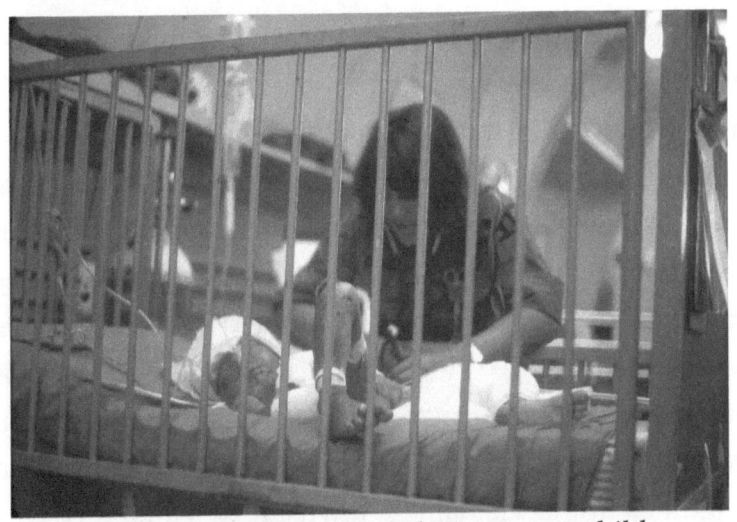
Shirley treating a wounded Vietnamese child.

The 8th field hospital in Nha'Trang was one of the smaller hospitals in Vietnam, and though Shirley didn't see as much trauma as was seen later in Chu lai, it was the place where she learned many new life-saving skills and was promoted to First Lieutenant. In addition to treating the freshly wounded, there was also a large ward of soldiers who were in the healing process, after having shrapnel metals dug out of their bodies. These guys were wounded, yes. But in a matter of time, they'd be able to walk and shoot again and that meant they stayed in Vietnam to heal.

The only guys who ever got evacuated from the hospitals were the ones with no hope of returning to battle. The ones who had had their feet, hands, legs, arms, or buttocks blown off, or more likely a combination of all of those. Maybe their eyes or ears were now missing, or too much flesh had been burnt from their bones. Or maybe, if they were one of the lucky ones, they'd been wounded three times in battle, but not badly enough to incapacitate them. If they got hit by the enemy three times and lived to tell about it, well, that got them a ticket home. Many soldiers in Vietnam fondly adopted the sentiments represented by three little letters, FTA (f**k the army). This emotionally charged acronym was often heard spoken between brothers in arms and was seen spray painted on buildings in the Vietnamese towns. It was a kind of way for the men and women of the Army to cope with the brutality they were surrounded by daily. Though many of them actually enjoyed their jobs in the Army and would later say that they missed being in the armed forces, at the time, it made them feel better to have someone to blame for all of the carnage (Downs, 2007).

    Life in Nha'Trang required all the doctors, nurses, and medics to not only become accustomed to serving injured and dying men, but to do it under harsh and unfamiliar conditions. The Vietnamese monsoons were unrelenting, and the Americans were always looking for cover. Everything they did, they did in the rain. Their equipment, their patients, and their coworkers were always soaking wet, and unfortunately, emergencies didn't wait for fine weather. They were constantly performing complicated medical tasks in less than ideal conditions, but no one ever seemed to complain. It was just part of everyday life in Vietnam, and Shirley quickly figured out how to thrive at her job in spite of the constant rain. Knowing that the soldiers' lives depended on their efficiency helped the medical servicemen and women to overcome many obstacles when it came to weather.

Shirley was assigned to the morning shift during her first month at the 8th field hospital, and each new day, as she would stand in the doorway of her barracks, boots laced and poncho in hand, she would look toward the mountains and think about the soldiers. She would imagine them staring up at the same sky and cursing the rain, a fierce distraction that could get them killed.

Pictures formed in her mind of them crouching between the trees, sinking in the mud, and concealing themselves from their ruthless enemies while the storm raged. As the raindrops pelted the ground in front of her, making small puddles, she envisioned some of the guys opening their mouths to the heavens, hoping for some clean water to drink. It seemed like each minute that passed, the downpour grew heavier, and she desperately hoped that some of them were able to wash their faces and catch some water on their tongues. It always reminded her of how many boys she had seen stricken with intense illness due to drinking dirty water. She leaned against the doorframe, looked down at her boots, and listened to the dampened wind.

This had become her routine, to stand in the doorway each morning, looking out at her new world, thinking about those she would soon be serving, and saying a prayer for them all. After a few moments of silence, she checked her wristwatch, realizing that the time had come for her to journey through the rain to begin her 12-hour shift. She pulled the poncho over her head, cursed the rain for the boys in the field, and took off across the base. Running didn't really seem to help her stay dry because she was always drenched upon arrival to work, and though she knew it didn't make much of a difference, she ran anyway.

In addition to the constant nuisance of working in wet conditions, the women of the Army Nurse Corps were learning to get familiar with the sounds of distant bombing, foreign tongue, and suffocating jungle heat. Though she was not marching out in the field with the soldiers, she fought one of the same battles that every man and woman on that war torn soil had to fight: The battle of the mind. It was nothing like Ohio, and Shirley knew she must adjust her outlook on life if she was going to survive the next year under such harsh circumstances that she was faced with everyday.

She thought about her past, the obstacles she had already overcome, and her new hope in God. Belief in an end to one's trials is a powerful tool of the mind. And so she chose to have faith. To believe that she would make it through the year. To believe that the soldiers would make it too. Whether they went home to their families, or home to their God, she had hope that they were all going to find peace and rest at the end of this. And so she prayed with them, and she prayed for them. She didn't know what else to do, surrounded by such misery, than to have hope in her newfound faith that one way or another, suffering would come to an end for each and every person who found himself or herself living or dying in Vietnam.

Living with Barb and knowing that they would be together through whatever they may face in war gave Shirley great comfort. They could share their hardest moments with one another, and they could find ways to make each other feel light too. They became each other's family over there, and together, they chose to remain strong for the boys in the field. They encouraged each other, and loved each other through the hard things they were seeing and they tried to make their time off seem as normal as possible.

The girls decorated the walls of their wooden barracks with a few posters they had brought from home and stashed their personal items in the footlockers sitting at the end of their beds. They both knew they were doing a good thing, serving the US boys who had been drafted into the war, and with that, at the end of long, eventful days, they were finally able to find some rest.

Work at the Nha'Trang field hospital had never stopped throughout the night, though. Foot soldiers didn't wait for daylight to try to kill one another. So in the morning, as rested as a new nurse could be, Shirley put on her jungle fatigues, observed her moment of silence and ran through the rain to switch off with the night shift nurses.

Though the US would be leaving the 8th field hospital in a matter of months, the workload stayed constant. There were lots of soldiers who needed continued care and attention in order to heal properly, as well as new emergencies coming in on an almost daily basis. With the pace of incoming injured men to the 8th field hospital, young Lt. Harbers was able to learn a lot about what her job would entail over the next year. As much trauma as she was seeing at the 8th Field Hospital, it wouldn't even come close to the volume of patients she would see later during her time in Vietnam.

She received lots of practical training and application back in the States by the Army, prior to being placed in the middle of a deadly war, and while it was actually a heavily emphasized piece of her education, the two places just couldn't be compared. Shirley enjoyed her training back in the States and thought the Army did a good job educating her, but she also realized that there was absolutely nothing that could prepare any man or woman for war except war itself, no matter how much it was talked about beforehand.

Being a nurse in the States and being a nurse in the war were two extremely different realities. As the weeks went by, working in Nha'Trang, Shirley began to understand that her career as a nurse would be forever changed by her experiences in Vietnam. She knew that if she could survive her first year as a nurse at war, then she would be able to survive any situation a nurse may face back home.

In the Nha'Trang hospital, Shirley learned first-hand how to do many procedures that she would ordinarily never have to do. In the States, under normal conditions, nurses wouldn't have to do things that a doctor should do, but in Vietnam, with so many men coming in freshly wounded from the battlefields, nurses were performing tasks beyond their training. For instance, nurses weren't supposed to give tracheostomies—they had never learned how to do it in training—but in the middle of the war, when bodies were coming in screaming and doctors were rushing around barking orders, Shirley learned to do what they asked.

She was a brand new nurse, and almost everything she learned, she learned right there on the spot. Much of the time, the nurses, medics, and doctors worked in teams, so she was able to watch and learn from the older and more experienced medical staff who were working alongside her. They all had one common goal... save the G.I.s' lives. The men and women around her helped Shirley perfect her craft, taught her new skills, and encouraged her to pursue excellence.

This was fantastic training for Shirley. She picked up the new skills quickly, mastered them in little time with minimal assistance, and became one of the most reliable, steady-handed nurses in the hospital. By the time she left Nha'Trang, she was knowledgeable, efficient, and dependable to make good medical decisions for patients. She was thankful to have been able to work with such skilled doctors and nurses at the 8th Field Hospital, and she knew she owed a lot of her new knowledge to these inspiring individuals.

Though it was tough to see the guys come in so injured and helpless, she was thankful to be one of the ones to get to serve them. One of the ones who could give them hope and possibly one of the people who would save their life. That's how she viewed it. It was a privilege to serve the boys, many of whom did not volunteer to be there. She tried to imagine what it would be like to receive the news, that just when you've become an adult, your country requires you to go to war. To not have a choice about putting your body in harm's way, to not have a choice about career or future. For many of the boys, news that they were drafted marked the beginning of the end of their young lives, and they knew it. These thoughts bothered her, as it did many people and that's why she volunteered.

She wanted to use her skills to help those unfortunate boys. She went so that others may live.

Besides being a skilled nurse, Shirley also had a great knack for bedside manner with the G.I.s. Being a newly devoted Christian, she wanted to make sure she treated every man with the dignity and kindness she believed he needed and deserved. She even began sharing her belief in God with those who were dying, as well as those she served with, without seeming pushy or self-righteous. In her heart, she believed in a love and a mercy and a saving grace that could get them all through this war, and being surrounded by such calamity, death, and finality of souls.

She wasn't sure if everyone had the chance to meet with the clergymen or go to the chapel and she felt she must share her newfound hope with those around her. Many of them were searching for something bigger to believe in, longing for rest for their troubled hearts and minds. Shirley had a quiet manner and a gentle way with her words, and she quickly became one of the most respected nurses in her unit.

It wasn't long before the Harbers family, back in Cincinnati, Ohio, received a letter from Shirley, in which she shared that she was being moved from the hospital in Nha'Trang to a different hospital at a military base called Chu Lai. Shirley decided when she left to serve in the war that she would open up communication with her family again. She wrote to them periodically to let them know where she was and what she was doing in Vietnam. Shirley's mother had even begun to send care packages to Vietnam with things Shirley missed from America, like peanut butter. Shirley let them know in her letter that she had received her new orders, along with Barb, to go work in the emergency room at the 91st evacuation hospital. She finished up her last days at the Nha'Trang field hospital, and vacated the premises along with the rest of the US military. She had only been in Vietnam a couple of months, but had learned so much, had become somewhat familiar with her surroundings and daily tasks, and now she was moving to a new home away from home. She felt a bit nervous all over again, and hoped she would find some peace at her new assignment. She thanked God for Barb, as they had become each other's piece of home, and together, they made their way to Chu Lai.

GOOD MORNING, VIETNAM!

Shirley in the ICU at the 91st evacuation hospital in Chu Lai, Vietnam, 1970.

Chapter Three

IT DON'T MEAN NOTHIN'

Michael was the youngest of two boys born to Helen and Edward Hensley. He had a brother, five years his senior, named Terry. They moved all over the country when the boys were young, but eventually planted roots in Ft. Lauderdale, Florida. Michael's father was a very well respected journalist for the local newspaper and his mother was a secretary for the local law enforcement agency. This left Mike and Terry to fend for themselves quite often, which at their young age, they didn't really mind. Mike enjoyed having the freedom to play with his friends and explore their surroundings, something he probably wouldn't have been able to do with more strict supervision.

During the summer of 1962, when Mike was eleven years old, he and a friend decided to trek through the woods near their homes and see what kind of fun they could find. They had just begun to play with matches and were enjoying lighting small things on fire and watching them burn out, making sure the fire was completely out before moving on to their next venture.

As they continued to make their way through the woods, they came to the edge of an unfinished housing development. There, they found and explored an abandoned house that was in terrible condition, and looked as though no one had lived there for years. It was fun going in all of the old rooms and imagining they were in a different world. They walked through the house, looking through some of the dusty artifacts for treasures. It was moldy and musty and overgrown and an awesome place for two young boys to investigate.

At some point, they found a wad of fabric and thought it would burn quite nicely. Mike stuffed the fabric up into a wooden corner near the ceiling and together, they lit it on fire. They watched in awe as the filthy rag went up in flames, giving a bright burst of energy and then dying out. When the rag ceased to be on fire, they lost interest and left the house to return to their homes for the evening.

When Mike went into his house, he looked for Terry to see what he was up to and found him on the back porch. Terry was standing, looking toward the woods at something that seemed to be of interest. Mike followed his gaze and when his eyes saw it, his heart jumped into his throat. Billowing black smoke rose over the trees and Mike's stomach tied itself into knots. A massive fire was consuming the abandoned house he had just left, and he could now hear sirens on the street. He froze in place, eyes wide, jaw hanging open, fixated on the fire. Terry noticed that Mike was acting strange, and knowing his little brother had been gone all afternoon, he asked him what he had done.

Mike confessed immediately, telling Terry that he didn't mean to, that he was only playing with the matches and thought the fire had gone out. He pleaded with Terry to understand that it was just an accident. Mike began to get panicky, his mind frantic as it played out all the possible consequences he would face for his actions. He finally concluded that he would most likely get arrested and go to prison for the rest of his life.

With these thoughts in mind, he begged his older brother not to tell anyone. Terry didn't tell anyone, but being the older and more responsible brother, he did talk Mike into turning himself in. He thought eventually Mike would get caught anyway, and it is always better to turn yourself in before that happened. He also, being a teenager, knew that Mike was not going to go to prison or get arrested, and it hadn't even crossed his mind that his little brother was afraid of those things. He simply explained to Mike that it was the right and honorable thing to do. After their conversation on the porch, Mike agreed

IT DON'T MEAN NOTHIN'

to tell the police what had happened and take whatever consequences may come.

The police, having worked alongside both Mike's mother and father, thanked Mike for telling the truth, and told him how dangerous and irresponsible it was to be playing with matches. After their stern talk, they let him go free.

Mike couldn't believe it! No handcuffs, no prison cell! Maybe his life wasn't over after all. Turns out, the place needed to be torn down anyway and since there was no other harm done, Mike's parents didn't even have to pay a fine. Mike knew he was lucky to get off the hook with such little trouble, and decided that telling the truth felt a whole lot better than keeping secrets. From that point on, he thought he'd live his life more carefully and try to stay out of trouble.

Every now and then, Mike's father would take the boys out with him to report on crime or accident scenes. The police would call him and ask him to come take photos of the scenes. Since they didn't have dedicated police photographers, they would use his photos for their case files. They liked Edward a lot and had a good professional relationship with him as a news journalist. Edward always did his best to tell the stories accurately and never added any extra drama or fluff. He simply reported what he saw, and the police appreciated that.

If the boys were home when a call came in, Edward would tell them to jump in the car and start loading his camera with film. He mostly took the boys on traffic accident calls. At a very young age, Mike and Terry saw first hand the devastation that a car accident could cause. Upon arrival at the scenes, sometimes even arriving before the police, they would find bloody people, crunched up vehicles, and even mangled and dead bodies lying on the pavement. Edward never told the boys not to look at it. He let them see it all and used them as assistants with his camera gear. The boys would help their father photograph the scene, following him around like shadows and blinking in the horrors of death and bodily dismemberment.

They boys looked on with admiration as the police would help those who were still living. They saw policemen jump into action to pull people from cars, to hold them as they lay in shock on the pavement and try to comfort them as they struggled to hang on to their weak life that was left after an accident. Both Terry and Mike thought they were heroes. Those guys didn't care if blood got on them and they did everything they could to help people they didn't even know.

Growing up going to these types of scenes left a very deep impression on the Hensley brothers. They learned to have a serious respect for driving a vehicle and knew how one mistake behind the wheel could cost them everything.

IT DON'T MEAN NOTHIN'

And they also gained a profound respect for police officers, for the heroes who woke in the middle of the night to help those who needed saving.

Mike's relationship with his father was confusing. While he saw his dad doing some really impressive investigative and undercover journalism, he also saw him drink and smoke himself into oblivion quite often. There were cigarette burn holes all over the house in places where his dad frequently sat, and he seemed to always be lightly squeezing a fresh cig between his fingers, yellow skin and fingernails completing the look. Maybe it was his way of dealing with all of the difficult things he'd seen.

One of the stories his dad broke to the public was about a mental health institution abusing its patients. Edward went undercover to live inside the asylum as a mentally ill patient, all the while recording the mistreatment he saw and received. He was able to expose the organization and its abusers and have the place shut down. Mike thought it was such a cool thing that his dad did. He was impressed that Edward made such sacrifices for the good of others but wondered why he couldn't stop drinking for his family.

When Edward came home from work, no matter what kinds of stories he had been working on for the day, he would sit in his white vinyl chair, and pound beer after beer after beer until he was gone from reality. Even the few times Edward took the boys on a trip up to Ohio, stopping for some adventures in the Blue Ridge and Smoky Mountains, they always had to stop to get a six pack of beer for the road. Sometimes Terry would drive, even though he wasn't old enough for a license, just so Edward could drink in the car. Mike would look out the window in the back seat, enjoying the mountain scenery and Edward would drink and pass out in the passenger seat, if he wasn't awake looking for another bar they could stop at.

Mike saw the inside of seemingly every bar from Ft. Lauderdale to Ohio, and found things he liked about each of them. The neon bar signs were one of his favorite things to spot at the bars. Sometimes they had the same signs as other bars, and sometimes he would see a new one he hadn't seen before. They'd move or be filled with glowing liquid. He thought they were pretty cool. He'd eat the greasy food with Terry while his dad sat at the bar, and then Terry would drive them further north until the next stop, usually a budget motel on the side of the road. There wasn't much money to be spent on these trips, and Mike's parents fought about it. Edward would conclude that he was taking the boys up to Ohio to see family, and Helen could choose to come or not. She never did. She would stay home and work, and Edward would take the boys to see his parents.

Mike and Terry didn't mind the old, run-down motels. They'd get out of the car and see a large hill, which they called mountains, behind the motel and Edward would let

IT DON'T MEAN NOTHIN'

them have the freedom to go climb it. They would run and hike up the hill together, getting out their pent-up energy, as young boys needed to do, and then they'd crash in the room just for the night before hitting the road again the next morning.

On one occasion when Terry was behind the wheel, Edward sleeping beside him, he couldn't figure out how to use the emergency brake as they were gliding downhill, picking up speed. The regular brakes didn't seem to be working, and Terry didn't know what to do. He was able to rouse his dad awake by pulling on him and screaming his name, just in time for Edward to wake up and pull the emergency brake, saving them from crashing into the side of a mountain. Terry felt the weight of responsibility heavily resting on him as he tried to keep them all safe, knowing all too well what car accidents could look like in the aftermath.

On days when Mike's dad didn't drink and smoke in the white chair, the family would go to The Tuna Bar just down from their house for the remainder of the evening. Helen and Edward would get off work and bring their boys to the bar, sit them down in a booth, and get them a soda and some food. Then they'd find seats at the bar together and drink beer and smoke for the rest of the night.

Mike would get his homework done at the booth, inhaling the secondhand smoke and munching down something fried for dinner. They frequented The Tuna Bar so often that all the regulars and staff knew their names and their usual orders. They were such loyal patrons to the bar that when Mike participated in a local soap box derby, his dad helped him paint "The Tuna Bar" on the side of his car. The bar was sponsoring Mike for the race and helped the family get the supplies to build the car.

Another patron of the bar, who claimed to be an ex race car driver, even spent hours in the Hensley's carport, helping Mike build the car. When race day came, Edward was the reporter covering the event. A photo of Mike in his Tuna Bar car made the front of the article. He came in tenth place overall, out of several dozen racers. He was pretty proud of himself and thought it was cool that he and his dad had something to bond over. When his dad was asked to go cover the national soap box derby in Akron, Ohio, he took Mike with him on the trip.

Mike didn't mind The Tuna Bar too much. It was what happened afterward that was so upsetting. His parents would start yelling at one another, usually about how little money they had and whose fault it was. Edward would get into a rage after all of his drinking, and their voices could surely be heard by the neighbors. Mike and Terry would retreat to their rooms and try not to listen to the arguments. Mike never knew if they laid hands on one another during these screaming battles, and he didn't want to know. He would try his hardest to ignore the fighting and go to sleep.

IT DON'T MEAN NOTHIN'

Helen wanted more out of life. She wasn't happy in their little mediocre house, with their mediocre jobs, and only having The Tuna Bar to look forward to. She loved the boys, but she wasn't the kind of mother to be super involved in their lives. Limited interaction with her kids was best for her both mentally and emotionally. She wanted luxury and expensive clothes and social status. She wanted to be somebody special. Somebody to know. Somebody who was somebody. Not just another housewife and working mother, married to a drunk and spending every night at the Tuna Bar.

This was her third time being unhappy with a life she had built, or rather, fell into. It was her third husband and second set of kids, another job, another city. It was a whole different life from the ones she'd left behind, but the happiness it brought her in the beginning was fading. Just like the other times. She felt she needed to keep searching for that perfect life that seemed to elude her no matter how hard she tried to find it.

She had two sons with her second husband and had battled polio while being a new mother. She had been hospitalized for having a nervous breakdown during that time and signed away her rights as the parent of her first two children while in the hospital. Many years later, one of those sons died in a car accident.

Helen desperately wanted to be happy, but didn't know how to be. She felt she had to keep searching until she found the key to happiness: keep changing her circumstances and surroundings, and maybe she'd happen upon it. But her life never turned out the way she thought it would. Love never lasted, money always seemed in short supply, and kids were much tougher to care for than she was emotionally equipped to handle.

The neighbors felt sorry for Terry and Mike. They had come to notice that the boys were often left alone, and when their parents were home, the shouting matches were long and loud enough for them all to know what was going on. Some of the neighbors tried to make up for what their parents were lacking. One guy across the street always invited them over to watch Friday night boxing with him. Mike loved it! They'd watch the battles, commenting, hooting and hollering together over the fights, and then sometimes, the man would take the boys to get ice cream afterward. Those were great nights for Mike.

Other neighbors stepped in to help watch the boys while their parents were off working or doing their own things. They'd feed them, buy them treats, and invite them over to play with their own kids. Sometimes the boys would end up staying long stretches of time with neighbors while their parents were gone. Eventually Helen and Edward started paying a teenage girl named Joni to come and nanny the kids so they could have even more freedom. But once Mike hit third grade, they didn't want to pay Joni anymore, and figured the boys were old enough to take care of themselves from then on.

At eight and 12 years old, the boys were their own babysitters. No more nannies or grownups to help them. They had to figure it out on their own. They cooked for themselves and learned to use public transportation to get around. Helen had subscribed to the Rich Plan, a monthly mail order service for food. At the beginning of the month, the boys would get the delivery, and it felt like Christmas morning! They'd eat all the things they liked in the first couple of weeks, Terry often doing the cooking for them. By the end of the month, there was nothing good left, and they'd be scraping by on whatever they could try to make a decent meal out of.

Mike learned that money was a huge deal in life. He wasn't quite sure why yet, or how to go about getting more of it, but he knew that his mom controlled the money, and every morning she would give his dad five dollars for his day at work. That would buy him lunch, a beer, a pack of cigs, and whatever else he might want while at work. He would often complain about the five dollars, wanting to take more, and she would try to explain to him that they couldn't afford for him to spend more than that in a day.

On a special night of the week, Helen would give Terry and Mike a dollar each to go have fun at the local shopping plaza down the road. They'd walk together, quite a ways, to the shops, making sure to keep track of their dollar. First, they'd go to the Royal Castle burger joint, and buy two greasy and delicious burgers each. Then they'd each get fries and a birch beer, and when they were all done with dinner, they'd have enough change leftover from their dollar to visit the drugstore and buy some candy for dessert! It was an amazing treat, when that special night came around. Even though Mike didn't know much about money, he knew dollars were important. Just look at what he could get for one!

For Mike and Terry, life took turns being grand and awful, depending on the moods of their parents, and the boys came to accept and expect that inconsistency was their consistency. They anticipated and predicted with great accuracy the ups and downs and they decided to be fine with it. Their parents would fight, and it was terrible and then they'd make up the next day and life was good again. Only, one morning, there were no apologies. Just a hard and short conversation. Mike, just 12 years old, found out that his parents were getting divorced, and he was to stay with his mom while Terry was to go with his dad.

Terry was sixteen by this point and knew someone would need to care for his dad. He would get a job, make an income, and take care of Edward, all the while having the freedom to do what he wanted. At seventeen years old, he asked his parents to sign consents for him to enter the military a year early, and they both did without hesitation. A year later, he was gone.

IT DON'T MEAN NOTHIN'

Mike didn't understand, and he asked why it was all happening, but he didn't get any answers that made sense to him. It was just the way it was going to be, and he had to accept it. His dad and brother would be moving out, to a different city, and Mike had to stay with his mom. His young brain couldn't handle the turmoil, and he retreated to his room to work out the mess in his own way. He thought about how his family would never be the same, how he didn't really have a family anymore, and the tears made their way down his cheeks.

He decided that he wanted more out of life too. He wanted a real family that loved each other. A family that stayed loyal to one another and liked each other. He wanted to be wanted and loved and needed and delighted in, and he was heartbroken that his family wouldn't give that to him. He briefly wondered if he'd ever see his brother and dad again, but then concluded he would. Even if he had to wait until he was a grown up, he'd find them and see them again. With that settled, and his energy already zapped from his emotional morning, he fell asleep, tears continuing to wet his pillowcase.

Shortly after the split, Helen began a relationship with her boss, whom she had been working for as a personal secretary for several years. His name was Allen Mitchell, and he was the sheriff of Broward county. Mike was impressed that he was the sheriff, but other than that, didn't feel any connection with him. Helen told Mike that the quality of their lives would be better with the sheriff, and after that, Allen started coming over to stay the night. Sometimes Mike would spend nights alone at home, as his mom never came home from work, and he knew that he was officially, totally, and completely on his own. He felt like baggage to the sheriff, baggage to his mom's next new life.

Allen was never mean to Mike, but seemed indifferent toward him. Mike felt tolerated. Like he was part of the package deal that came with dating Helen. Eventually, they moved out of their tiny duplex and into Allen's nice, big house in Plantation, Florida. Helen told Mike he would have better opportunities there—the high school would be better, and his life would be better. Mike didn't have a choice, and once the move happened, he felt as though he were just renting a room from them. They had their separate lives, and he had his, alone.

His mom saw him as old enough to get by on his own, and she was now living the life she always wanted. Fancy dinner parties to get dressed up for, local politics, status, more money, though not a lot more, but she was finally somebody—the sheriff's main woman, and later, the sheriff's wife. It was all that she dreamed, and she couldn't be happier. However, the many lives she lived to make it to this point still took turns playing their memories in her mind's eyes. She concluded that she was as happy as she was ever going to be, and she settled into life with the sheriff.

She loved her kids, but didn't have to take care of them anymore or have too much interaction with them. She could be proud of them from a distance. She traveled to foreign countries, wore fine clothing, and started modeling. Her life was turning out exactly how she always thought it should've been from the beginning.

Mike had some contact with his brother and dad after the divorce, but it wasn't much and a lot of it was second hand. His mom would say she talked to Terry and update Mike on his life; she would relay information about Mike to Terry as well. Before Terry joined the military, he kept extremely busy taking care of Edward and working.

Mike saw Terry as an inspiration. He had a job, was making money, had a girlfriend, and seemed very independent. Mike couldn't wait to do the same. The one time Mike did visit their apartment, he saw his dad sitting in the white vinyl chair, drunk and smoking cigarettes, and Mike thought it was as if no time had passed at all. There was no progress being made with his dad turning into a more responsible man, and Mike started to understand why Terry had to go with him. Edward truly did need to be taken care of, and Terry was doing it.

When Mike got settled into the sheriff's house, he went looking for a job, and thought he'd start where Terry used to work—The Palmland Printing Press. They did all the print material for the sheriff's office, so Mike figured with Terry having worked there and now that he was living with the sheriff, that he had a pretty good chance of getting the job. He did. It was the first time in his life he was making money, and it felt so incredibly good to feel even an ounce of independence. At fourteen years old, he worked at the press every Saturday for a dollar and a quarter an hour. He loved it! He started buying some of his own clothes. Seeing how his mom valued fashion so highly, Mike thought it was important to always look and feel good in whatever clothes he was wearing. She had taught him that fashion was important and that clothes said a lot to people about who you were and where you were going in life. He took this advice to heart and was even voted best dressed his senior year in high school.

He also saved a lot of the money he made, and by the time he was sixteen, he bought his first car—an old junker that was on its last leg, from a used car salesman who just happened to be his uncle. Uncle Marv treated Mike as he would any Joe Schmoe off the street. No family discount, no deals, over zealous in selling the hunk of metal.

Mike was just happy to have freedom, a set of wheels that would run where he wanted them to go. Uncle Marv was Helen's brother and made out well financially with all of his used car dealerships. He had a nice house where he hosted his sister's marriage to the sheriff. Helen and Allen were married in August 1967. Mike attended the wedding, happy that his mom was so happy, but still feeling like an outsider to her new family.

To mind his own business and let the happy couple pretend they didn't have a kid, Mike would spend many weekends surfing with friends at the beach. He installed a rack on the top of his old, red Renault and would strap his surfboard on top every Saturday.

Hugh Taylor Birch State Park was the usual meetup spot. He loved the water and the freedom he would feel out in the waves, sun shining down on his face. The ocean was such a place of simultaneous adventure and solace, that Mike decided to get his scuba diving certification. He took his courses at the Naval Diving and Salvage Training Center. From that point on, he could be found in the water. He'd bring both his surfboard and scuba gear to the beach and shore dive reefs, surf the waves, and relax in the sun, all in a day's fun. He was a Florida boy through and through.

When he wasn't at the beach, he was either studying in his room or working. Mike was an excellent student, an aspiring doctor, taking the more difficult classes his high school offered, including advanced courses in latin, biology, and physics. He liked his teachers, his guidance counselors, and his books. Learning was already an obsession, and he was good at it. His counselors and teachers believed in him and gave him the confidence to declare his desire to practice medicine. Out of that spoken desire, Mike began to choose a path that would lead him to greater knowledge in the medical world.

He soon discovered a job opening at a local funeral home, T.M. Ralph Funeral Homes. Mike was thrilled to move to a more interesting and exciting job. He didn't care much for the funeral side of the job, but he loved the medical side. The hearse doubled as an ambulance in Plantation during the sixties, and Mike was the medical attendant in the back.

When a car crash happened, the funeral home would get a call from the police. Mike and the driver would rush to load up the stretcher and the oxygen tank and place the red light on the roof, transforming their hearse into an ambulance! Mike had basic first-aid medical training that he learned from Mr. Ralph's first aid class at the funeral home, and as a sixteen-year-old kid, he did the best he could to save the lives that so happened to end up in the back of his hearse. He mostly administered oxygen and tried to stop bleeding while they sped to the hospital.

He enjoyed being on the rescue so much that on the weekends he would spend the night at the funeral home, sleeping on a cot just one room away from the embalming room, so that if calls came in the middle of the night, he could ride in the back of the ambulance.

T.M. Ralph lived above the funeral home with his family. They were Catholic and had many children. Mike would always see the kids running around and playing while he was at work. Tom Ralph taught Mike to always wear a white dress shirt with a tie and bring a coat when going on calls. If the patient didn't survive the accident, Mike was instructed to offer condolences to the family and hand them a card for T.M. Ralph funeral homes. Having been the vehicle to already have carried the deceased to the hospital, they would hopefully be chosen by the family to provide services. Mike didn't enjoy that part, but knew it was the way of the world. People live, people die. And the family needs someone to take care of the embalming, the cremations, the coffins, and the services.

Sometimes Mike would assist Tom when embalming bodies. As he drained the blood and replaced it with formaldehyde, Tom always had a cigar in his mouth to combat the pungent odors. Mike handed him instruments throughout the process and helped fill in cheeks and lips using small syringes, so they didn't become too concave or deteriorated looking. Family members would come in to choose a coffin, and Mike helped them decide. When it was time for the funeral, Mike would greet guests and have them sign a book of attendance for the family. It was a good job and for a little while, Mike considered becoming a funeral director just like Tom Ralph.

Around school, Mike started to be known as "Doc." The other kids knew he was a first aid responder in the ambulance and respected his important job and specialty skills. One night while hanging out at a house party, classmates came running over to Mike calling out, "Doc, doc!" They brought him to a girl who had taken a hard fall and landed on her head. Mike looked her over and figured she probably had a mild concussion. He ended up driving her back to her home so she could be with her parents and rest. He enjoyed his nickname and the respect from his peers that came along with it.

By the end of high school, Mike had made up his mind that he was going to do what Terry did and join the military. He figured he would get drafted anyway, and if he just went ahead and enlisted, he'd have a better chance of choosing his course. Still wanting to pursue a career in medicine, he figured he could sign up to be a medic and get some free education while earning a paycheck and serving his country all at the same time. He didn't have the money for college and neither did any of the adults in his life. While Helen was enjoying the lifestyle that came with Allen's paycheck, that money was reserved for the two of them, not to be spent on Helen's son's education.

The military seemed like his best option, and he thought he didn't have much to lose if things didn't work out in his favor. If he survived his four years, he'd have a great educational foundation for medical school, money saved up, and he'd be eligible to use the G.I. Bill to help pay for higher education. The week after he graduated from Plantation High School, Mike walked into an Army recruiter's office and enlisted. Just a few weeks later, he

IT DON'T MEAN NOTHIN'

was off to basic training in Columbia, South Carolina at Fort Jackson.

The week leading up to his departure, Helen and Allen decided to take a trip to Europe. Perhaps they were unaware that their eighteen-year-old son was going to miss them and would have liked to spend his last week at home with them. Maybe he would have even liked for them to take him to the airport, to see him off and say good-bye, that they'd miss him and wait anxiously for letters. He'd never live under their roof again, and he had kind of hoped his moving out, his launching into the real world, would have been a bigger deal to them.

They hadn't thought of any of these things, and if they had, they didn't care enough to change their plans. He hadn't realized how much he was still trying to belong to the only family he knew, until he was so stung by their absence.

Neighbors Colonel and Darcy Morgan stepped in to give him the ride to the Miami airport instead. They often came on the scene when Mike's parents were busy with other important things. Mike was thankful to have a ride and for someone to wish him luck in his new life. It wasn't his parents, and while that would've been nice, at least it was someone.

He was dropped off at the Miami airport early on a June morning of 1969, and he spent the next thirteen hours filling out paperwork and being properly processed as the newest property of the United States government. Those poor Florida boys who had either been drafted into the service or had, for one reason or another, actually enlisted, finally landed in Columbia, South Carolina around 10:00 pm. These young kids were just starting the first day of their new life, unfortunately for many, a life that was cut very short by war.

"This is a bunch of bullshit . . . Will write soon if they give us time. Must go because I have to hurry up and wait again . . . Love, Michael" His first letter to his mother from the United States Personnel Center, Fort Jackson, South Carolina. It was written underneath a pre-typed letter from the Army, letting parents and families know that their loved one had arrived safely and not to write them at this address, as they would soon be leaving the processing center for a more permanent address with their basic training unit.

In his first real letter to her, the one where he was given enough time to write all that he had wanted, he reflected on his last week at home alone and considered it to be well spent. "I went around and said goodbye to my friends. At night I was usually busy with a date. On the last night I went over to Sam's house for dinner and took her to see 'Romeo & Juliet' . . . it was a sad night."

Mike thought his first week at Fort Jackson was absolute hell. The boys were given their clothes and I.D. cards, stuck with various immunization needles, and given new

IT DON'T MEAN NOTHIN'

haircuts and weapons. He felt like the Army treated them like they were nothing. Nothing at all.

Over time, once he got used to the processes and procedures of strict military living, he came to accept his new life and began to make friends. One evening Mike was invited to play cards, a game called acey-deucey, where players guessed if a certain card would fall in-between two dealt cards. Mike got sucked into the game, hoping to recoup his losses each new round but ended up losing his entire two-week paycheck in one night. He felt sick about it and wrote a letter home to his mother to tell her how stupid he had been and that he was never going to gamble again.

During basic training, Mike rose quickly to the top of his class. He scored the highest marks on his written exams, shooting, and physical fitness. He was promptly promoted to a squad leader and enjoyed the recognition of his high performances. Toward the end of his eight weeks at Fort Jackson, he was actually starting to like the military and already felt like he was headed down the road to success for his future. He had asked to become a medic and was granted the opportunity. After a thirty-day leave at home, he would be transferred to Fort Sam Houston in Texas to receive his medical training. He felt he had made a good choice choosing the military and was well on his way to becoming a doctor.

Mike's graduation from basic training.

Mike came home from basic training, sporting his uniform, looking older and even more handsome. He had grown up a lot in eight weeks—more fit, more mature, and more knowledgeable about his country, his freedoms, and definitely more patriotic. He was dating a girl from his hometown and discovered that her father had just given her a beautiful and powerful muscle car. They decided to take it on a date one night, and she wanted to drive. At one point during the trip, she wanted to show off its power to

Mike and slammed the pedal to the floor. Mike watched in horror as the engine roared and the car, completely out of control, careened through a concrete building straight ahead. Mike's left ankle was fractured in the crash, but they were both okay.

Since he had been on leave from the military, he went to get patched up at an army clinic. They put him in an ankle cast, and he had to use crutches for a while. He never dated that girl again.

His leave came to an end, and though he was still recovering from the ankle injuries, Mike boarded a National Airlines flight in Miami slated to land in San Antonio. Shortly after the plane took off, while the passengers were eating breakfast and enjoying coffee, Mike noticed the stewardess being walked hastily toward the cockpit, a man behind her, holding a gun to her back.

He couldn't believe his eyes, and his mind began to race with options. Ever since he had donned his full military uniform and become a trained soldier, he felt the weight of protecting the people, but he wasn't sure there was anything he could do to stop what was happening. He wondered if he could grab the gun from the man without getting anyone hurt. Before he could come to any conclusions, the man and the stewardess were at the cockpit in what seemed like no time at all. Mike leaned forward to warn the woman next to him, who hadn't been paying attention. She started to panic and as more passengers became aware, a foreign voice came over the intercom. The man explained that the plane would not be landing in Texas that day, that instead, they were going to be taking a detour. He informed everyone not to worry, that no one was going to get hurt. All of the passengers became very alert, and as the plane took a sharp turn off course, they began to realize what was happening. The plane had been hijacked, and they were going to be landing in Cuba.

Mike watched out the window as the plane made a sharp turn. The plane soared south and as they came over land, Mike noticed the large sugar cane fields below and dozens of green jeeps with the communist red star on the top. When the plane touched down, it bumped and bounced violently, the pilot slamming on the breaks to try to stay on the runway. It was a very dangerous landing in Cuba, and the bigger jets had quite a difficult time trying to stay on such short runways. Mike and the other passengers were thrust forward, hitting the seats in front of them, being tossed from side to side and colliding with one another. The rough landing made Mike think that maybe they were going to crash. The plane finally halted, and, within no time, dozens of armed soldiers filed onto the craft and told everyone to get off the plane.

Immediately Mike began to feel all eyes on him and one other young gentleman, also wearing his United States military uniform. He knew his situation wasn't great but

IT DON'T MEAN NOTHIN'

all he could do at that point was hope for the best. When the Cuban soldiers got to Mike's row, they stopped, observed his uniform, and very sternly told him to sit right where he was.

Mike was beginning to worry but was able to remain calm. After all of the civilian passengers were off, the soldiers came to retrieve Mike and the other US soldier, and took them to a small, dimly lit room. After a few moments, they were separated, and Mike was interrogated by the Cuban military.

Mike sporting his US Army uniform.

An officer asked Mike questions in broken English about the United States military, about missiles, military secrets, and attack plans. They were very intimidating, making threats and acting like they might start torturing him for more information.

Mike gave them his name, rank, and serial number, as he had been instructed to do if ever captured and taken as a prisoner. He told them he had just gotten out of basic training weeks ago and knew nothing about any of that. They tried to get him to tell more until they realized he was telling the truth. His youth, rank, and undecorated green uniform supported his ignorance on the topics and after what felt like days, they let him off the hook.

All in all, they held him in that dark room and interrogated him for eight hours. Though it was exhausting and somewhat nerve-racking, Mike stayed pretty calm on the surface throughout the whole ordeal. When they decided they were finished questioning him, they loosened up their tough guy acts a little. They brought him freshly brewed espresso, a sandwich, and just before the main interrogator left the room, he reached into his pocket, pulled out a coin and flipped it across the table to Mike. He might have even had the slight hint of a smile on his face, as if he were giving the young American kid a souvenir for his troubles.

Mike picked up the coin and examined it. It was a Cuban nickel. He stuck it in his pocket to keep forever, thinking that maybe one day he'd have kids and grandkids to show it to.

Eventually all of the passengers were loaded back onto the plane, flown back to Miami and then on to San Antonio. When Mike arrived at Fort Sam Houston, he had to debrief with military officials, which didn't take long since Mike hadn't even known any information to tell the Cubans. The local newspaper wrote an article about the hijacking that named Mike as a passenger.

The cuban nickel Mike saved from his interrogator.

Hijacking planes to Cuba was not uncommon during that time. For some, it was the only way they could return to their home country and to their families, since the United States enacted a travel ban to Cuba. Others were making demands for political asylum in Cuba, and still others were the result of terrorism, extortion, and mental illness. It seemed that the news stations were reporting about a new Cuban hijacking every week.

Eventually all of these disruptions spurred the two governments to come to an agreement and write new laws. In 1970 both countries signed new laws that recognized the hijackings of planes and maritime vessels as a criminal act. The law outlined terms for hijackers to be returned to the United States for trial or prosecuted in Cuba for their crimes. The United States also started taking preventative measures to crack down on hijackings by having airports install metal detectors in 1973. (Mazzoleni; Catusi, 2019).

Once all of the fuss about the interrogation was squared away, and with his ankle fully healed, Mike could settle in at Fort Sam Houston and start focusing on his specialized medical training. He had elected and been chosen to be trained as a surgical technician, a 91-Delta. He still wanted to become a doctor and knew this higher level medical training would be a great way to continue down his desired career path. As a surgical tech, he would get advanced medical training, get to work directly with doctors, and learn how to perform complicated and life-saving surgeries.

Medical training lasted for six months since Mike had to go through both the basic medical training and then the surgical technician training. He enjoyed what he was learning and had a great aptitude for practicing medicine. He made new friends and they hung out in their barracks or went out on the town after classes were over.

IT DON'T MEAN NOTHIN'

One night he decided to walk from the base into town alone, and on his way back home, he saw another young guy across the street walking the same direction as he was and just a few paces behind him. Mike felt uneasy about the guy—he looked like trouble to Mike, but at the same time Mike didn't want to overreact. He kept an eye on the man and decided not to think too much of it until he noticed that there was another guy on the same side of the street, walking directly behind him. They started to pick up their pace, the guy from across the street crossed over and Mike's suspicions were confirmed. They made their move, running up to him quickly and grabbing him from behind. They rummaged for his wallet and one of them struck Mike over the head with something hard. He fell to his knees but held onto his consciousness.

From the ground, something inside him burst to life, like an angry animal becoming uncaged. He somehow was able to fight his way free from the two men, and his instincts told him to run. He took off for the races toward base, and they were both chasing after him. All of his military conditioning paid off, and the thieves never caught up to him.

He ran all the way back to the base, went to his room, and collapsed on his bed. He had escaped robbery with his life and his wallet. He felt satisfied that they got nothing from him, but that feeling that his life had been in grave danger didn't leave him for days. He told all of his friends, and they thought it was pretty cool he'd escaped and outrun them both. He had a big knot on his head where he'd been clubbed to prove his story. He never reported it to police or his superiors, but wrote home to tell his mom what had happened.

From Fort Sam Houston, Mike was transferred to Fort Stewart for one year. It was there that he picked up smoking cigarettes. He would watch all the other doctors, medics, and nurses take breaks from working and enjoy a coffee or tea and a cigarette. It looked relaxing, and it looked cool. Soon enough, he was joining in. He was really starting to enjoy military service. He'd been exceptionally successful since basic training, becoming a squad leader quickly and passing all of his physical and intellectual exams with the highest marks. Many of his medically trained friends were receiving orders to go to Germany, Japan, and all over the world. He hoped for somewhere interesting, with great hospitals so he could continue to learn even more about being a surgical technician. It was at the end of his time at Fort Stewart that he received his next set of orders. Vietnam.

When he read the orders, he was a bit surprised and caught off guard. Feelings of fear and apprehension washed over him. He hadn't requested to go to Vietnam and was really starting to believe he may make it four years stateside or at a hospital somewhere else in the world, somewhere having a time of peace.

IT DON'T MEAN NOTHIN'

He stared at the word on the page: Vietnam. All kinds of thoughts made their way to his mind. He had never been out of the country before, and Vietnam was half the world away. He thought that becoming a surgical tech might save him from Vietnam orders, might make him more valuable, more eligible to get sent somewhere else. No matter what he had thought, he was accepting the fact that he'd be going to Vietnam for a year.

He was granted another thirty-day leave to go home and say goodbye to all his friends and family. His mom and Allen were busy traveling and attending community events, so he went on vacation with his girlfriend, Sandra, and her family to New York. While there, his girlfriend's older sister, Susan, urged him to desert to Canada, to evade his orders and stay alive. She told him he was going to die over there and to avoid being part of this war. She pleaded and begged him to let her take him to the border so he would live a long life. She told him that he really didn't want to go over there; it was nothing but bad news. They all knew of so many boys that went to Vietnam and never came home.

He understood that her wish for him was out of grave concern and respect for his life and he appreciated that someone cared so much that he stayed alive.

Mike never even considered it, though. He didn't want to go to Vietnam, and he certainly didn't want to die, but he was not a deserter. He was not a coward, and he was not a runaway. He learned a long time ago that it's better to face your fears than to run and hide from them.

He told Susan that there were a lot of young men over there that didn't want to be over there, and they were relying on people like him to save their lives. He had made a commitment and he was going to follow through with it. He knew being sent to Vietnam was a risk when he signed up, and receiving orders to actually go didn't change anything. He also already knew he wanted to be a man of his word: honest, trustworthy, loyal. No matter how long or short his life might be, he would live it with integrity. He would go to Vietnam, and he would do what he had been called to do.

The more he thought about his deployment, about the other young men, many of them drafted out of their lives, away from their hopes and dreams, plucked from their futures, and forced to go and live the last year of their young lives humping through the bush and being barbarically attacked, the more he wanted to be with them. He knew he had specialized training. He knew he could help, he could save lives, he could offer hope to those boys.

As Vietnam drew nearer, his motivation and his attitude about going to war changed. He was not going just because his orders commanded it. He was not going because he believed in this war and all of its political agendas, to stop the spread of communism, or because his country needed him. He was going for the other soldiers.

IT DON'T MEAN NOTHIN'

He was going to do everything in his power to save them. To save their limbs, their breath, their futures, their lives. He was going so that others may live.

Chapter Four

A WARM WELCOME

Mike first stepped onto Vietnamese soil at the military base in Cam Ranh Bay, toward the end of June, 1970. On the journey over, he had looked around the cabin at all the other soldiers. He knew in a year's time all of these men would be sorted into different categories. Some would be KIA (Killed in Action), some would be missing limbs, some would just be missing altogether. And for some, they'd still be alive and physically intact, but he was sure even for those ones, there would be lifelong emotional wounds. He sat there looking around, wondering what category he would fall into next June, hoping against the odds he'd be one of the "lucky" ones.

Everyone else was undoubtedly wondering the same things and hoping for the best outcome. Sadly, many of those men's wishes and dreams, their futures, would soon

A WARM WELCOME

be extinguished. It was scary to think about fate on that flight and eventually it ended up being better to just not think about it. To carry on as if life were normal and one was only starting a new job.

It had been a long flight from Seattle, and as they finally arrived at the war, clean, well-nourished, and rested, they noticed a long line of men standing near their plane. These guys were scruffy, scrawny, and tired. Mike thought they looked like hell, and was surprised to see their wide smiles. They weren't smiling at the new boots filing off the aircraft though, they were smiling at the actual aircraft. They had somehow, by the mercy of God, survived their year's deployment to one of the most deadly wars for American soldiers in history, and they were finally going home. They were getting on that plane as soon as it was empty, and they'd never have to look back. The higher the rank, the closer to the plane they were, and as Mike and the rest of the guys continued to file off the plane, the old-timers began to hoot and holler.

The new guys walked by them, hardly able to meet their eyes. Some of those dirty soldiers had sad eyes, despite their smiling lips, some of them looked angry, some of them looked sorry for Mike, and some of them hurled insults at the new arrivals. They called out things like, "Short-timer" and, "You're not gonna make it" as they grinned wide at their plane and patted each other on the back.

Feeling disheartened, Mike continued to walk in line, following the other new arrivals. As he did, the surviving soldiers kept howling their doom. Daring the new boots to survive their year, demanding respect from them, for still being alive and standing after 12 months. All of them looked old, beyond their years. It didn't really scare Mike, but he didn't particularly like seeing them either. He wondered why they had to see each other, the guys on their first day and the guys on their last. He knew some of them he came over with, would never see that day. They'd never be in line, waiting for the new guys to vacate the plane that would take them home. They'd never get to stare at the clean guys and command respect with their eyes, just for surviving. He knew he might even be one of the ones that would never see that day. It seemed wrong.

Being in Cam Rahn Bay felt like being in basic training again. Gone were any feelings of individualism he had gleaned in the States from his completed first year of service, where he had gained a little independence, respect from others, and even had his own room. Arriving in Vietnam, it was back to being just another number, just another grunt. Back to being herded around with many others and having a group mentality. He didn't like the way that felt, like he was starting over at the bottom, but like so many other times in his life, he quickly got over what he knew he couldn't change and followed his orders.

A WARM WELCOME

It seemed like Mike spent half a day waiting in long line after long line at different stations, getting assigned to his orientation group, receiving his OD (olive drab) green jungle fatigues, and given a barracks assignment. He was also assigned to Alpha Company, First Battalion, 46th Infantry Regiment in the Americal division (1/46th Americal, for short).

The barracks where Mike was to stay for the duration of his in-country orientation was his first experience with sheer and utter misery in Vietnam. Being placed on the top bunk of a three high bunk bed in those sweltering steam rooms, also referred to as quonset huts, was a disadvantage. Lying down to sleep that first night, he could feel the heat emanating from the ceiling. The semi circular huts were not very tall, and being on the top bunk, he could reach up and touch the ceiling from his lying down position. He stretched his hands up to feel the corrugated steel, just feet away from his body and immediately yanked them back down. The ceiling was so hot it burned his hands. Cursing that the huts were made of galvanized steel, he pressed his body as deep as he could into the thin, industrial mattress, desperately trying to escape the ceiling heat.

As sweat poured over his entire body, the sand that was already in his bed stuck to his skin. For some reason, sand seemed to be everywhere and on everything. There was nothing he could do to keep it off his bed, or off himself, and everyone was dealing with the same miserable combination. Over-sweating, overheating, and being constantly coated in sand. It was not the kind of warm welcome Mike would've liked. Exhaustion took over and he eventually managed to sleep that first night in spite of how miserably airless the room seemed.

In the morning, Mike quickly jumped down from his cot, and after showering away the sweaty sand, he dressed out in his olive drab fatigues and reported to the bleachers. He found his spot on the green wooden bench, crowded in next to all of the other new arrivals, and waited patiently for everyone to get situated.

The officers who were conducting the orientation began to make their speeches and the war rookies listened intently. The officers told the young soldiers to always watch their backs, to keep in mind that just because they were on a military base, it did not mean they were safe. This was war and they needed to keep a keen eye on their surroundings. Bases had been bombed, and that's why they would learn to run for the bunker when the alarm sounded, warning of incoming rockets.

The young men felt uneasy and nodded to each new warning they were given, consuming the alerts like medicine. They all desperately wanted to survive their year and each bit of advice seemed like a treasure to hold onto. Mike thought it would be a miracle if he ever made it home.

A WARM WELCOME

In the middle of his thoughts, just as everyone was sitting on the bleachers, a loud explosion went off from underneath! Interrupting the officers as it detonated, the blast sent panic and chaos tumbling through the young men on the bleachers. Mike instinctively covered his head and crouched low, as did those surrounding him. After the initial noise died down, the guys looked up to see the officers standing calm and smiling at them. They were not wearing happy smiles, however, but the kind a person wears when they've just taught someone a horrible truth.

"You're all dead," the officers explained. The bomb was a blank. It had been their first lesson in becoming paranoid. The officers drilled in the fact that they were not safe and would never be safe as long as they were in that God forsaken country.

Though they were fighting alongside the South Vietnamese ARVNS, it was extremely difficult to tell their allies from their enemies. Oftentimes, Vietnamese would pretend to be ARVNS or simple villagers when they were actually "Victor Charlies" or NVA. This allowed them to spy on troops from peaceful villages or sneak onto Army posts and US military bases, plant bombs, or even become suicide bombers (known as Sappers during the Vietnam war).

In essence, the new guys learned that it didn't matter where they were or what they thought they knew about someone else, they needed to know to never trust anyone but a fellow American. This was particularly hard for some of the guys who were attracted to their hooch maids.

Hooch maids, or mamasans if they were older, were women from the nearby villages who would come onto the military compounds, clean the barracks and do the laundry for a small fee. While some were older women, roughly the age of the young mens' mothers, many were beautiful, young Vietnamese women. Though they smiled and maybe even flirted with the Americans, it was possible that they could be dangerous. Besides the fact that they operated with a high rate of theft, some of them could possibly be NVA sympathizers living in the South.

The guys were warned that if they weren't careful, one of their mamasans or hooch maids might plant a bomb right in their barracks. Though it was extremely rare that these women had ill intentions, the guys knew that they should keep their wits about them, even around their hooch maids. The same was true for the village children. The GIs loved playing with the kids and giving them candy, but they never quite knew if they might pay the ultimate price for it. What may look like an innocent young boy could actually be an enemy soldier. Paranoia at all times was the ticket to survival.

Mike committed to himself that he would keep a careful watch of his surroundings all the time. The officers had been successful in embedding their possibly life-saving paranoia mentality into the new guys. Over the next

A WARM WELCOME

couple of days, he learned more about what his year was going to be like and became convinced that if he was careful enough, he would survive. He would make it to the end and be waiting in line to get on that plane.

At the end of orientation, feeling overwhelmed by information and looking forward to getting his job assignment, he stripped down to his underwear and climbed onto the top bunk. Though he felt completely sticky and the small space between his body and the boiling hot steel was almost perfectly suffocating, he went to sleep with a small sense of happiness knowing that it was his last night in that nasty place. He only hoped his next barracks would be a step up from this one.

In the morning, he grabbed his Army-issued duffel bag and reported to his transfer location. A giant vehicle sat on the far end of the runway, in OD green, it's back ramp lowered to the pavement, it's chunky wings outstretched. Along with the others, he climbed into the large C-130 plane, furnished with hanging mesh nets on the sides, for seating. He settled into his spot, facing across the center aisle at the other young soldiers starting their 365 days of deployment. Three days down, 362 to go, and his countdown had begun. From Cam Ranh Bay, they were headed north to the US Army Post called Chu Lai, on the coast of the South China Sea.

Shortly after taking off, they skidded to a halt on the metal runway in Chu Lai. As they disembarked from the plane, each young man went about his way, finding his new barracks, or platoon.

Mike took in the surroundings of his new home, scanning the post and imagining what horrors he might experience in this place over the next year. He felt uneasy all over again and doubt about his survival began to creep back up to the surface of his mind. The sounds of mortar rounds going off could be heard coming from the bush. He also heard the uniquely identifiable sound of Huey helicopters, which were flying overhead, taking off, and landing in droves.

Huey was the nickname given to the Bell UH-1 Iroquois military helicopter. The first time these copters were used in combat was by the US Army during the Vietnam War. They were designed by Bell Helicopter in 1952 to meet the requirements for the Army's medical evacuation and utility helicopters.

At the time, their current choppers were too large, underpowered, and too difficult to maintain to serve as MEDEVAC (medical evacuation) vehicles. Bell developed the new, lightweight, single-engine aircraft with double main and tail rotor blades, which gave the Hueys their distinctly recognizable "chopping" sound. Throughout the course of the war, the UH-1 was continually modified to meet the various needs of the troops. Some were tasked with ground-attack or armed escort roles, and these were promptly outfitted with rocket launchers, grenade launchers, and machine guns. These "gunship" Hueys were given nicknames such as "Frogs" or "Hogs" for the ones with launchers and just simply "guns" for the ones outfitted with machine guns.

Bell also designed a special gunship, still in the Huey family, but better suited for ground attacks. The guys coined these special crafts as "cobras" or "snakes." The MEDEVAC and troop transporting Hueys became known as "slicks" because though they did usually have door gunners, they were stripped down to allow maximum body capacity. More than 5,000 Hueys served in the Vietnam War (Clark, 2002. Klimek, 2021).

As the Hueys continued to soar overhead, Mike shielded his eyes from the sun and looked up to catch a better glimpse. He had never flown in one before but was pretty sure he'd have a few chances to do so in Vietnam. As the choppers went out of sight, he made his way to the check-in tent, to get registered and finally start working.

Having been specially trained as a surgical technician, Mike was very surprised and unhappy to be told that the hospital did not have a need for him. The Army claimed that they had enough surgical techs already at the hospital but were short handed in other areas. So instead of doing the job he had trained for, he was given orders to spend the next 12 months manning the small clinic on the outskirts of the post.

Feeling somewhat reluctant, but knowing he had no other choice than to obey the orders, he grudgingly reported to his duty with feelings of great disappointment. He thought about how hard he had trained for the past six months, and it was upsetting to him that he would not get to help in the way he had imagined. He came to save lives. To work with doctors, to assist in life-giving surgeries, he came so that others may live. How could he be given such a seemingly non-essential role when he had been through advanced training? He was a Specialist 4 (SPEC 4). Feeling that old familiar way, like mere property of the US government, he canned his disappointment and began working in the small, one room building.

The Chu Lai clinic proved to be a boring job, but at least it was a job that felt relatively safe. It was better than humping through the bush, but he really wanted to use his specialized training to do the most good for those guys. Being in the clinic just felt like a waste of his knowledge. It was something a 91 Bravo could do, a basic medic, the ones out in the platoons. For someone like Mike, coded as a 91 Delta, with intense amounts of highly skilled training, the clinic just didn't seem like a good fit. He figured the Army wanted someone with advanced training to be in control of the clinic, but he didn't care, he was quite upset to not be utilizing his education.

An overwhelming feeling of discontentment crept in, as he spent more and more time at the clinic, and he knew

A WARM WELCOME

that somehow he must try to make a change. Nevertheless, Mike worked diligently through his shifts, trading off with the other medic, 12 hours at a time. The little clinic was about 12 by 20 square feet, and it only needed to have one man working in it at a time.

The walls had tiers of shelves lined with all kinds of medicines and supplies. Platoon medics would come see Mike, standing behind his half door, and get resupplied for the battlefield. Sometimes when a medic would come to the door, fresh off the battlefield, perhaps on a one or two night break from humping through the bush, Mike would look at the poor guy's tattered and bloodstained clothing and his unshaven face and feel a sense of gratitude that at least he wasn't out in the bush. Although at other times, he looked on these medics with a sense of naive jealousy, feeling somewhat useless working at the small clinic and wishing to do something more helpful, something that made a bigger impact, a greater difference. He didn't come to Vietnam to stand behind a half-door and hand out supplies from his safe little room. Not that there were actually any safe places in Vietnam, even on military bases, as orientation had taught him and as he would later find out ... but still, relatively safe compared to those guys out in the bush.

Over the first few weeks, he got used to seeing the infantryman come in out of the jungle. They were dirty and they were in bad shape. Sometimes worse off mentally than physically. The war had gotten to them, to their fear. Some of these guys had seen too much, had come too close to death, and now that they were out of the bush, they desperately wanted to stay out. Maybe some of them were just days away from completing their 365 day deployment and had become paranoid that they'd be killed in their last week. These ones would come to the clinic, show their battle wounds, and beg Mike to code them as not being fit to return to active duty.

Many times, he could not comply with their requests, because physically, they were okay. Other times, he would send them on to the hospital and let the doctors make the final decision. He did not want to be the one in charge of making those kinds of calls, and as he would explain to his young peers that he couldn't help them in that way, his hands would rise, palms forward, as if to say, "I'm innocent. I am not the one with the power to make you go to war, and I am not the one who can bring you out of it."

He hated those moments, but he tried not to let it get to him. He knew he needed to focus on two things: his current job, and getting a new one.

The most action young Specialist Hensley ever saw at the clinic was when a soldier would come out of the bush with jungle rot, also known as a tropical ulcer. It would either be in his feet or sometimes in his crotch, and would have to be examined. On these occasions, Mike would have the soldier come inside, remove his boots or drop his drawers accordingly, and upon inspection of the problem, Mike would dispense the proper medication, or send the poor fellow on to the hospital if it had progressed to a more serious state. The problem was that there was just so much moisture. It was in the air, from the monsoons during the rainy season, from the intense humidity during the dry season, and from the endless bouts of perspiration seeping out of their pores. It was nearly impossible to prevent this type of infection from happening when these guys lived outside for weeks or even months at a time, many of them never removing their wet boots. Because of their lack of hygiene in the bush and endless amounts of insect bites, even the smallest abrasions could turn into the most afflicting forms of jungle rot. If not properly taken care of, the jungle rot could worsen and lead to much bigger problems like bone infection and even amputation.

The heat was so intense in the bush that these guys blew right through their water purifying tablets in no time and were forced to drink unclean, standstill puddle water. This water was filled with bacteria and caused fierce spells of dysentery. When men are hunting each other for the kill, something like dysentery has to be put on the back burner, to be worried about when they return to a base and can visit a clinic, if they survive the bush.

Some guys had it so bad that they ended up ripping the crotch out of their jungle fatigue pants, to allow the mess to run down their legs as they hiked. As disgusting as it was, it became a preferable alternative to allowing the sickness to pile up in the seat of their pants. There was no such thing as stopping for bathroom breaks in the middle of a war. A simple step off the trail, or the sound of a zipper could get a whole unit killed if it so happened in the wrong place or the wrong time (Clark, 2002).

Medicine for dysentery was stocked high and full in the little clinic, and it was the one most frequently distributed by Mike. It seemed like everyone who came in from the bush was suffering from it. Over time, the irritation Specialist Hensley felt as he continued to dole out medicine and supplies, as well as examine the occasional jungle rotted crotch, spurred him into action. From his little clinic, he could see across the base and into the distance about a half a mile away, the 91st evacuation hospital. He knew it was where he belonged, and he became determined to find a way to work there.

One day after getting off work from one of his 12-hour shifts, he decided to visit the doctors of the 91st. He was curious if he might see an opportunity to move jobs, to be able to do what he came for, which was to assist with surgeries and help save lives.

Mike Hensley was confident, well-trained, academically sharp and best of all, good-natured. In no time, the doctors took a great liking to Mike, and once they found out he was trained as a surgical technician, they

A WARM WELCOME

were on the move. The doctors were appalled that Mike had been told the hospital was well-staffed and didn't need him. They were, in their own professional opinions, under-staffed and could greatly use a skilled technician like Specialist Hensley.

Mike was glad to have them on his side and hoped that they'd be able to get him reassigned. He thought about all of his time in training and how he was beyond ready to assist in surgery. He had about eleven months to go in Vietnam, and it was hard for him to imagine spending all of them stuck in that small clinic.

The US Army doctors, especially the ones drafted right out of their American private practices and thrust into war, far away from their families, had a lot of clout in the military politics in Vietnam. They went on behalf of Mike to the right people, requested him by name, and within a few days he had received new temporary orders to report to the 91st evacuation hospital as an Operating Room (OR) surgical technician.

This was exactly the outcome he had hoped for! When he went to thank the doctors of the 91st, they told him they were sorry that they could only get him temporary orders, but it was the best they could do. It didn't matter to Mike though, he was elated to be moving on and moving up, taking steps in the right direction to do what he came for.

When the man in charge of making sure the clinic was well staffed found out what Mike had done, he was furious. Enraged that Mike had gone over his head, he threatened the young specialist that with only having temporary orders he'd get him assigned right back to the clinic in no time. Mike was sorry to have upset that man, but at the same time, all he cared about was getting into surgery, helping to save the G.I.s' lives. Mike promptly finished up his last shift at the small clinic, packed up the contents of his foot locker and moved into his new assigned barracks, right next to the hospital.

Mike sitting on the chapel steps near the 91st evacuation hospital in Chu Lai, Vietnam, 1970.

Chapter Five

CHINA BEACH

Work at the 91st evacuation hospital happened in 12-hour shifts, and the doctors, nurses, and medics would be assigned to either the day or the night shift. Shifts ran from 7 am to 7 pm, or 7 pm to 7 am, but always 7 to 7. The type of shift they were given would last for one month and then they'd switch to the opposite hours.

At the turn of their individual month-long cycles, they would get a full 48 hours off to accommodate for a sleep day. This way they could effectively reset their bodies to switch from day to night shifts or vice versa, which was extremely important, as these people were the medical professionals responsible for performing surgeries and saving the lives of patients who could not afford to have mistakes made. Working 12 hours a day, 6 days a week was exhausting. They may not have been sleeping in the jungle, or stepping on bouncing bettys, but they were seeing the worst of the worst of the war, every single day. It was both physically draining and emotionally taxing. On their one day off they would have the opportunity to visit the local orphanage to teach English or they could hang out on the coastal cliffs with their comrades, watching the South China Sea rise and fall and try to find some sense of peace.

Shirley was getting used to her new routine in Chu Lai, and she was enjoying it more than she had in Nha'Trang. Though her new barracks were much closer to the 91st evac hospital than it had been at the 8th field hospital, she kept her morning tradition of waking up early, standing in the doorway, and saying a prayer for the soldiers out fighting in the bush. She'd pray for their safety and for their families back home, for the doctors and nurses, and for God to help her do her best work that day. Then she'd run the short distance through the rain and begin her 12-hour shift in the intensive care unit (ICU).

As she made her way to the hospital one oddly sunny and dry morning, she took a moment to briefly scan the post and the new scenery. What she saw was remarkable! The sand meeting the sea, masses of land jutting up out of the earth to her east and jungle strewn mountain ridges to her west. Being from Ohio, she was not accustomed to seeing beaches and she couldn't help but think just how beautiful it was to see the sunrise over the sea. She thought the beaches in Vietnam were breathtakingly gorgeous.

From the base there was a steep, rugged path down the coastal cliff to the shore. To get to this tiny patch of sand, people had to carefully climb down the rocks. Once down at the beach, there was access to the water, though it was rocky and could be dangerous when the tide was coming in. Making it down to the water was worth it for the soldiers, though. It was the place they could go to escape the everyday horrors of the hospital and sit alone, listening to the waves and praying for some peace.

One day a young medic decided to go down to the small inlet for a break in his day. Too much time had passed since anyone had seen him and when they went searching for him down by the coast, they found his lifeless body lying back in a rocky cave area where people liked to sit. He had drowned during an unexpected monsoon, which sent the South China Sea barreling into the rocks, with strong winds and forceful waves. Shirley thought it was such a shame to be dragged all the way to war, halfway across the world, only to die from something that should not have happened. She wondered briefly if his family received the same home visit by an officer as the other kids who were killed in action.

The Vietnam War was the first war that the US military changed it's KIA notification procedures. In past wars, families of the deceased had received telegrams in the mail, but beginning with the Vietnam war, the military became adamant about having an actual person deliver the news face-to-face. The military was already being criticized by their fellow citizens and knew that they needed to protect their reputation among their countrymen. This new way of notifying families in person, would help them show the families just how much their loved one's service had meant to the military, much more clearly than the impersonal telegrams of the past. (Ellis; Lade, 2018).

Shirley made friends quickly and easily when she got to Chu Lai. Though she wasn't stationed at the same hospital as Pat, whom she had known from Fort Campbell, they visited one another a couple of times and decided to join a small, informal Army band together that would allow them to sing at gatherings from time to time. Once, they even jumped aboard a huey for a lift to a LZ (Landing Zone) to sing for the arriving G.I.s. They were told to entertain the troops, and so Shirley, along with Pat and four other nurses did their best to be an encouraging sight to the new arrivals. They smiled at the young men, greeted them, and tried to engage them in small talk about where they were from back home.

It was comforting for the men to be met with friendly American faces, a small resemblance of home to help set their minds and hearts at ease. Shirley liked chatting with the young men, seeing them strong and healthy, and thought it was great that she actually got to do something fun with them. Shirley thought the G.I.s were so respectful of the women and were genuinely thankful that the nurses came out to welcome them to the country. Even though she only got to go out to a LZ one time, she loved the experience and would've done it more if she had been offered the chance.

Usually the nurses who sang together would go down to the enlisted club, situated near the enlisted barracks on the post, and sing on the small stage to provide some much needed entertainment. None of the nurses played any instruments, so their voices were accompanied by tape decks, powered by the generators.

Shirley really enjoyed this new venture, as it became a good way to meet more people and make more friends. Right away, the nurses got to know the guys who were in the professional Army band. They called themselves the Joint Chiefs of Staff, and their assignment was to play music. It was their whole purpose in Vietnam, their only job, and an important one. Their music boosted morale and drowned out the foreign sounds of the war with the familiar sounds of rock n' roll. These guys had a full set up ... drums, guitars, bass, amplifiers. It was the best escape from reality there was, short of drugs, and the enlisted club had a full array of liquors and beer available also.

In no time, Shirley and the other nurses who sang, including Pat, became good friends with the guys from the

Joint Chiefs of Staff. They became particularly close with the drummer, Wayne. He was quite handsome with blonde shaggy hair and a charming smile. Sometimes, Wayne would even invite the girls up on stage to sing along with them as the band played. He was a short-timer from the day they met him, only having a few weeks left until he got to go home. He was engaged to a woman back in the world and couldn't wait to leave Vietnam and get back to his real life in just a matter of weeks. That was the hard part about making friends in Vietnam. Everyone was on a different year-long schedule and it seemed like as soon as Shirley got to know someone, they were going home, back to the world.

Though Shirley never really considered herself to be much of a singer, she really enjoyed her time singing with the band and getting to serve the soldiers in another way. One of the things she liked best about it was that it was the only time she ever got to interact with the soldiers under happy conditions—a stark contrast to when she usually saw them, in the ICU.

Even though they were around such disasters all day, the nurses tried not to let it get to them. In fact, they could not allow it to get them down. Shirley knew this, and became really great at functioning as a nurse under very sad circumstances. She knew that the soldiers needed someone to take care of them, not pity them. There would be plenty of people who would do that for them later. Her job was to make sure that they would have the opportunity to be pitied. Her job was to be part of a team that was trying to save them. And in order to do that well, she knew she could not be affected by the blood, the missing limbs, the tattered skin, or the screams. She had to be her best. She felt that she owed it to the soldiers not to be sad, so she tucked it away, somewhere where it would not inhibit her professional abilities. That's what they all did. And after work, the music would keep the sadness at bay.

One day after getting off work, Shirley decided to walk over to the dentist office, which had been set up for the soldiers. She figured she might as well get her teeth cleaned, while it was free. As she walked through the front doors, she was greeted by a young man, smiling and extending a hand. His name was Dennis, and he was the dentist.

Right away, she knew she liked Dennis. He was friendly, personable, and seemed to be quite positive. She noticed he wore a wedding band, and she respected that he was a married man. After he checked her teeth, they sat chatting for a bit, and Shirley began to feel that perhaps he was becoming too friendly. She looked again at his gold ring, and wondered if it meant anything to him while he was over there. It didn't seem like it.

Being a brand new Christian, Shirley didn't hesitate to ask about his behavior. He smiled and flirted with her, and she decided to ask him directly if that was a wedding ring he was wearing. When he answered in the affirmative, she let him have it. Shirley was bold, but friendly in the way she let him know that she did not agree with his behavior. She told him how he had made a commitment to someone back home, his wife, and that he should respect that.

He didn't quite see it the same way she did, but he liked her honesty and genuine personality. Before she left, she asked him to think about what she had said. She smiled, shook his hand quickly, and was out the door before he could respond.

Over time, Shirley and Dennis became friends. He would be leaving to go back to the world before she would be, and Shirley desperately wanted to see him change his ways before that happened—to quit messing around with other women and recommit to his wife. They had many conversations about religion and God, and why he should be faithful to his wife when he was halfway around the world in the middle of a warzone.

Shirley shared her personal testimony with him—how believing in God had saved her life and how she found so much joy in knowing her creator. How she had hope for her future and believed in the principles of the Bible. By trying to follow the example of Jesus, she felt that she treated people the right way and that her life was fuller for it. She believed she had a greater purpose than personal happiness, that she was there to love other people well and share what she knew about God with others. She wanted him to be able to experience that kind of purpose and joy too.

After their conversations, Dennis always sat quietly, contemplating the ideas his new friend was sharing. Over the months, they had become pretty great friends, and Shirley felt as though he was really soaking it all in. It was just before he left for America, one night they had met at the officer's club, and Shirley laid it all out for him—everything she had been through in her past, all of the abuse she had suffered during her childhood and why she believed what she believed.

They went outside, under the stairs to get some privacy when Dennis made the decision that he wanted the peace she had. He wanted that hope, he wanted that kind of purpose that he saw in her, and her strength, and the morals and principles she had, he wanted it all. He wanted to have the power to treat other people, especially his sweet wife waiting for him to return home, better. He trusted that Shirley was right. That the peace and hope and joy she was talking about would only come with a relationship with God. He was ready to step into faith.

Shirley was delighted to hear all of this from him. Their friendship had grown so much, and it was almost impossible to believe that he was the same guy she had met so many months ago at the dentist office. Together, under the wooden stairs leading into the Officers Club, they prayed together. They continued to meet to talk about

God, the Bible, and how to conduct themselves in the middle of war, as Christians. Shirley was so thankful to have a Christian friend to hang out with, when it seemed that almost everyone else was doing whatever felt right at the moment.

A couple months later, Dennis came running up to Shirley at the mess hall. He was holding a letter in his hands, from his wife. Shirley noticed the joy that exuded from him, and she thought it was a beautiful transformation. He showed her the letter and wanted to read it to her. As he read aloud the words from his wife, Shirley got goosebumps. Dennis's wife had asked him in the letter to find Shirley and thank her for everything she had done, and for investing in Dennis's spiritual well-being. His wife said that when Dennis left for Vietnam, she started praying diligently that he would somehow come to have faith in Jesus while he was over there. When she had received Dennis's letter telling her all about his new faith a month ago, she almost fell over and couldn't wait to thank the person who had the courage to share their beliefs with him.

To Shirley, it was one of the happiest moments she had experienced in a long time. It wasn't much longer after that, and Dennis was gone, back to America, to his wife, and to his new life as a Christian. Shirley felt the loss of a close friend when he left, but she was so happy to have met him. She prayed that he'd continue down the path of learning more about God and that his relationship with his wife would be better than ever.

On her walk back to her barracks, she decided to stop into the Officers' Club. The Officers' Club was a special building designed specifically for Army officers to escape from the brutal reality they were faced with each day. It was on the very edge of the base, right on the rocky coast and had wooden stairs leading up to the doors. The entire thing was encircled with sandbags, which made it nice and dark inside.

The nurses would mingle with the doctors and other officers, dance, listen to music, and drink. For many, that was the best part of the club— the drinks. Shirley wasn't a heavy drinker but liked to wind down at the end of a long shift with a refreshing cocktail, some good music, and being surrounded by people having fun.

At the club everyone wore their civilian clothes, which added to the feel of it being a place where they could live normal life, even if only for a couple of hours. The nurses had fun ordering new clothes through the J.C. Penney catalogs for such occasions as going to the Officers Club or on their R&R trips.

Oftentimes, Shirley would notice that the doctors would be grilling steaks! They had special items flown in to them all the time, and steak was one of their favorites. The grill they were using to cook the steaks, was also flown in for them. The doctors had some impressive leverage in

Vietnam, and were able to get things like boats and skis. How they were able to procure all of these things was a mystery to Shirley, but she enjoyed some of the benefits of their extravagance. She ordered her usual, rum and coke, and sat down at a table. She gently sipped her cocktail, closed her eyes, and let the music take her away. She had big dreams for her future, joy in her newfound faith, and a lot of hope that the rest of her life was going to be good.

While Shirley was sharing her faith with Dennis, working backbreaking shifts, and grasping at whatever small respite the Officers' Club could offer, Mike was enjoying his new job at the 91st evacuation hospital. Over time, Mike became well known amongst the doctors and they were all glad to work with him as their assistant during surgeries.

Mike was not only skilled in his work, but he studied the doctors he often worked with and began to learn their unique styles of operation. He watched closely and made mental notes of the tools they gravitated toward for specific procedures and eventually was able to anticipate what the doctors would need and would hand them their tools before the docs even had a chance to ask for them. This made the doctors extremely happy and made Mike very popular to work with.

Though it was more difficult emotionally to see the guys who were in the OR, it was what he was trained for, and he was glad to be in a position where he felt like he was doing the most good he could possibly do for the fighting men. Though he absolutely hated seeing dying American soldiers, he knew he had made the right choice to move to the OR.

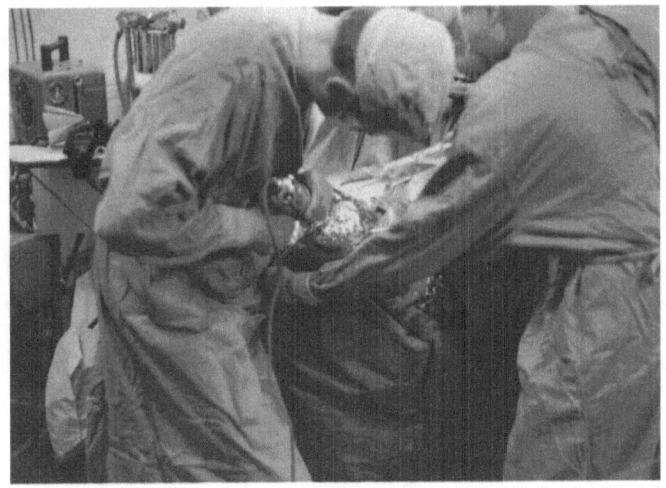

Mike operating on an enemy soldier in the OR.

Over the weeks and months, Mike became numb to seeing the fresh slaughter of war. They all did, and it was a good thing. It allowed them to focus on their jobs, to be steady handed and clear minded, to make life-saving decisions for the fatally wounded soldiers who lay upon their operating tables.

When Mike first started in the OR, he'd get pretty disheartened after spending 12 grueling hours trying to salvage lives that had been literally ripped to shreds. Everyone in the OR worked quickly, diligently, and with high levels of precision and intelligence. These were highly trained professionals and they had come to war prepared to see their guys butchered, and to fix them when possible. But still . . . it was never easy to see fellow Americans in such horrid shape. Mike knew the only way to be most effective and to serve the soldiers to the best of his ability was to push the emotions back, to keep them suppressed, and to perform the tasks that needed to be done.

Mike would bottle up the hurt he was feeling for the soldiers, and it would sometimes come out on the surface as anger. He was very angry, almost all of the time. He thought about how many soldiers he had lied to intentionally. They'd come in from the dust off (medical evacuation helicopters), in horrendous shape, and Mike would quickly look them up and down, assess the damage, and most of the time, he knew when they were going to die. The ones who were missing all of their limbs, or half of their head, or had massive gaping holes in their bodies.

Mike would try so hard not to let his face reveal to them their fate, but instead, he tried to stay positive for them. He'd tell them they were going home, getting out of that terrible place, and that they'd be okay. He didn't know what else to say, and so he tried to comfort them with what he thought would be words of hope. They were the hardest and most selfless lies he ever told. When they'd finally pass on to the next life, Mike would shake his head, tears burning just below the brim, and he'd look to the sky, furious at the helpless situation he was in, wondering how anyone could possibly believe in God.

Mike's anger would present itself in different ways depending on his circumstances. One day during brain surgery on an enemy soldier, Mike found himself standing over the table looking down at the tray to his side, which had a piece of the enemy's skull sitting on it. As he waited for the doc to operate on the young man's brain, he reached down and picked up the piece of skull, careful to maintain the sterile environment. He looked it over thoughtfully, examining the inside of the human head. Shiny black hair had been shaved away during the preparation for surgery, and Mike held the bald piece of skull in his hands, thinking about all of the crazy things he had seen since coming to war.

As he sat there waiting, human bones in hand, he suddenly felt compelled to leave his mark on the enemy. He reached down to the tray next to him, grabbed the scalpel and hastily decided to write something in the man's skull. Something for the bastard to remember him by. He wasn't quite sure why it felt like the right thing to do, but at the time, it did. And so, he went with his gut and began carving his initials into the man's bones: M.H. When he was finished, he flashed a mischievous grin at the doctor, who promptly returned the sentiment without a word.

When it was time, Mike handed the skull over to the doctor, who placed it back over the man's brain and reattached it to the rest of the man's head. To Mike, it felt like he did something good for the soldiers. Like he violated one of the violent attackers who was killing them, and he felt pretty proud of his quick thinking to do it while he had the chance.

He realized later that he must have been dealing with some pent up anger because carving in that man's skull brought so much satisfaction to him. He even took delight in sharing the story with others, stating that a Vietnamese guy would be walking around with Mike's initials carved into his skull for the rest of his life. It didn't hurt the guy, and Mike knew it was a minor blow, if considered one at all, since the man would never know. But still, it seemed to ease a tiny piece of fury that bubbled just beneath the surface. However small an act of revenge, at least it was something.

The more he thought about how good it felt to hate the enemy, the more he realized that he needed something to help dissipate the anger he felt. Something to help the feel of normalcy return to his heart. He didn't want to be an angry, bitter person, but the war was testing his mental strength. He thought about girls, how a relationship would be nice, or about maybe going to that orphanage he had heard people talking about. Maybe it would do him good to be around kids. The next time he had a day off, he'd check it out. But for the time being, he'd continue to smoke his pack a day and drown his thoughts with beer and rock 'n' roll.

On a particularly chaotic day at the 91st evac, Mike had just about enough of treating the enemy soldiers. He watched as his peers were carried into the OR on gurneys, mangled, disoriented, and calling out for help. The guys were blown to pieces, their open wounds filled with earth and metal, their skin jagged at the edges from being ripped open by shrapnel.

Many of the wounds were too large to close; gaping holes, missing skin. The best the medics and nurses could do for these poor men was to clean the jungle out of their bodies, flush their raw flesh with saline, and cover the openings with sterile gauze.

Oftentimes the guys had so much of the bush in their wounds, that they looked completely black with dirt. Sometimes it surprised Mike how wholly dirty these guys were coming into the hospital. He imagined they must've been standing directly on top of a mine—how else could the grass and earth penetrate so deeply into their bodies? Though it was shocking to see these wounded warriors come into their operating rooms, the medical professionals contained their pity, mentally blocked their anger, and did everything in their power to save the soldiers' lives.

Unfortunately, it was at times of high volume like this, that the hospital would be receiving men from both sides of the war. Americans and enemy soldiers alike. This was one of the most difficult parts of the war for the medical professionals. They would see their young countrymen come in, screaming, dying, and ripped to shreds, and they would do their best to save them. But when they were all finished taking care of the US soldiers, they would begin to care for the enemy. The enemy who was responsible for all the carnage they had just tried to fix. The enemy who put the American boys through such trauma with their torturous guerilla weapons. But because the American military operated above reproach by following the Geneva Convention, at least in the hospitals, these same doctors, nurses, and medics would go straight from treating US soldiers to treating NVA and VC. It was almost beyond human capability, but they did it. They did their jobs, they treated injured and dying men, no matter their creed. Though it came at a cost.

Anger would have to either be suppressed, sent deep down into the soul to fester, or find another way out. At the hospital, they played by the rules of war and provided treatment to every injured person who came to them. Sometimes it was easier to do than at other times. It all depended on the situation.

On one such day, after telling a young traumatized soldier that he'd be okay, encouraging him that soon he'd get to go home, and then watching him pass away as Mike knew he would, his hatred for the enemy bubbled to the surface. He was then told to go and operate on an enemy soldier who had been involved in the fight that just took place. The young VC was holding his left leg and howling in agony. Though there was a significant language barrier, there were two numbers that communicated quite well between the Vietnamese and the Americans. Everyone knew that number 1 meant the best, and number 10 meant the worst.

That young man looked up at Mike, pointed to his leg and said "Ow, ow, you make number 1." Mike looked down on the enemy soldier holding his leg and crying in pain. He knew the guy would survive; his injury wasn't life threatening. He also knew he had no other choice but to do his job and treat the man's leg. It was an oath he had sworn. To help the wounded, no matter who they were. It was just much more difficult to actually put it into practice. Knowing there was nothing he could do to avenge the death of the US soldier, Mike resorted to attitude. He picked up a wooden tongue compressor from the table behind him, held it up in front of his face, while making the cruelest, most hostile expression he was capable of, willing his eyes to exude hatred toward the enemy. He pointed to the enemy's leg and with great power yelled, "No! Number 10!" and with that, he snapped the tongue compressor in two and threw the pieces on the ground. He saw a brief look of fear creep over the young man's face, and it brought slight, temporary satisfaction to Mike. He then sedated the bastard and fixed his damn leg, because it was his job.

Any feelings of sympathy Mike could've possibly felt for this young man were long gone; they died with the young American he had just watched pass on to the next life in pain. He had once again lied to his brother in arms when he told him he'd be alright, and he knew the boy was dying, but he said it anyway. How was he supposed to know, at 19 years old, how to give someone the last words they'd ever hear? He'd choke back his feelings, hold their hand and walk alongside their gurney, desperately trying to comfort them with empty words, "You're gonna be okay, man. You're safe now. We're gonna take care of you, do everything we can for you. You're going home, man."

They'd medicate the fading soldier, hoping to give him some peace, some final moment of relief from the pain before his lights went out forever. It was the hardest thing to do.

In addition to being a surgical tech in the OR, Mike also had to work guard duty at one of the bunkers on the coast about once a week. Guard duty was something every enlisted man did, no matter what his job was. For Mike and the other medics, it was calculated into their 12-hour shift work. On guard duty days, the guys would work only eight hours at the hospital and then spend the remaining four hours manning the bunker, searching the coastal cliffs for intruders.

CHINA BEACH

It was a job that was too important to be done alone, so they worked in pairs. The bunker was quite comfortable, large enough for Mike to have his own space. It was a ten-by-ten foot square hut, with a slanted roof, a narrow opening at eye level all the way around, outfitted with large, hand-controlled searchlights on the corners. There were two sets of thick wooden walls, with a layer of sandbags in between to protect the guards from incoming fire, explosions, and shrapnel metals.

It felt pretty safe for what it was, and Mike didn't mind being there. He'd walk up the stairs into the spacious room, which was up on stilts overlooking the cliffs of the beach. He spent his four hours scanning the waters edge, up and down the shoreline, and keeping a careful watch on the LRBs out in the sea. LRBs were "little round boats," which were actually just floating baskets the Vietnamese fisherman would use to cast their nets and bring in the seafood for their village.

The fishermen were harmless and knew better than to come too close to the shore near the US Army Post. However, Victor Charlie wasn't overly concerned with US military rules and might try to use the disguise of being a fisherman to get close enough to the post to either physically breach the compound or fire a rocket in from one of the LRBs. Mike knew it was a possibility and took the job very seriously.

Shirley sitting inside a LRB (Little Round Boat) on the beach.

Each part of the post in Chu Lai had guards pulling duty at all times. The hospital, where Mike worked, was responsible for keeping an eye on the coastline they were situated near. All guard posts would be in communication with the central post command, checking in every half hour to report their findings. Mike would radio in when the time came and give the all clear. Armed with guns and radios, the guys knew they had permission to fire and call for backup if they ever saw anything aggressive happening near their shoreline. Though they were always worried about VC trying to climb up the rocks from the beach and break their secure perimeter, it never happened for the entire year that Mike was there. He was thankful to not see any action during his guard duty days. It was a pleasant break from the hospital, and though it had the potential to be more dangerous work, it was actually calming when nothing happened.

After a few months of writing letters home and waiting for a reply, Mike was extremely happy to hear that the USO (United Service Organization) would be visiting. That meant that the phone, which was able to call home, would be open for use. He couldn't wait to call home and talk to his mom, to let her know he was doing okay, and to hear her voice to know that she was doing okay too. He figured she was probably worried sick about him all of the time, and it would be great to talk to her. Unfortunately, by the time Mike got to the USO building, the line for the phone was already filled with soldiers waiting their turn.

He walked to the back of the line and patiently waited. Soon, many others were behind him, and he wondered why they didn't just allow them to call home whenever they wanted. Why did the phone have to be off limits, except for specific days here and there? The guys all knew there was a time limit of about five minutes, a common courtesy to those waiting in line. When Mike got in line, there were about fifteen people in front of him, and as he stood, fifteen more behind him.

As each soldier took his full five minutes, talking to loved ones back in the world, he thought about how great it would be to hear his mom's voice. He hadn't heard it in so long, and since he had left for Vietnam, he hadn't heard it at all. He may have been 19 years old, but he still longed to hear from his parents. After more than an hour went by, it was finally his turn to use the phone. All of his patience was about to pay off, and it would be worth it. He eagerly grabbed the phone, dialed home, and waited for the operator to connect the call. Immediately the sheriff, Mike's step-dad, picked up on the other end. The operator told him that she had a call for him from Michael Hensley, all the way from Vietnam! The sheriff then asked the operator if the call was a collect call. When she answered that yes, it would be a collect call, he told her that he did not want to accept the call, and he hung up the phone. The operator came back on the line with Mike and told him what had happened. Right away he hoped that the sheriff didn't think he wouldn't have paid for the call if he could have. They had to call collect, it was the only way!

He hung up the phone, after only about 30 seconds with it in his hands. His face flushed red, and his heart ached. Feeling completely deflated and confused, he walked away from the USO building. The others who had waited so long with him didn't say anything; they just watched him go. He was the only one who hadn't taken his five minutes, the only one to have his phone call home from war denied because it cost money. It was completely embarrassing and he couldn't believe he had wasted all that time waiting in that stupid line. For the first time in his young life, he had to face the reality of what he had known for years . . . he was on his own.

He had never felt so isolated from others in his life, and the more he thought about what had happened, the more it hurt and angered him. He longed to be part of something with others—a family, a community, unconditional acceptance and love. He had never known what that was like, but in vain, had tried so hard to believe he had that with his mom. Unfortunately, it just wasn't true. His family was broken, and she was building a new life with the sheriff, and he was just the extra baggage from her past—the way he had always felt but had buried deep down when he was younger. Now, it was right there on the surface, slapping him in the face, waking him up to the truth.

He finally accepted the fact that if he was ever going to find happiness, he'd have to move on. He had to find new people. A woman to love, hopefully with a great family, like his brother had found. He wanted it so bad, it hurt. In that moment, as he reached his barracks, he vowed to himself to be different when he had his own family. To love them wholly, completely, and fiercely. He made a promise to himself that his family would know without a doubt that they were loved, wanted, and accepted. With that thought in mind, he kicked off his combat boots and lay on his bed, dreaming of a happy future, believing he could make it come true.

Chapter Six

FORBIDDEN, HIDDEN LOVE

It was a humid weekend on the compound, when Shirley had worked her six days straight and finally had a day to rest. She could either go to her barracks and try to relax, or she could busy her mind with trying something new. The latter always seemed to be a better choice for her, so she decided to join the group heading to the nearby village of An Tan. There wasn't much to do around the base on days off anyway, so going to the village and helping with the kids sounded like a great idea. She was also hoping that it would make her feel like life was a bit more normal than it actually was. She had been hearing from other nurses and medics that volunteers were needed to teach English to the kids, and she thought it'd be a nice change of pace from her daily routines. For a moment, she could focus on a different kind of human need. That of a child needing love, instead of a soldier needing a miracle.

The deuce and a half truck took Army personnel to visit the orphanages of the nearby village every week, same day, same time. There, the soldiers could play with the kids and teach them English at the school. The more she thought about it, the more it sounded like exactly what she needed. She headed to the pick-up point and took a deep breath as she saw the armed cargo truck parked in the dust, waiting for everyone to board. She hesitated, thinking about the possibility of the driver having to use his gun to try and keep them safe once outside the compound. The thought was fleeting, and she figured it was unlikely they'd be ambushed trying to get to the orphanage. Plus there were units of men whose entire job was to clear the roads of explosives left by the enemy. She took one more deep breath to exhale the uneasiness, and with that, she walked confidently toward the truck.

Shirley climbed into the large truck bed, along with about ten other nurses and medics she had never met. As she sat there waiting to leave, she couldn't shut off her mind. She thought this would be a great opportunity to meet some new people from Chu Lai, like when she joined the band, and she thought maybe she'd even get to hear the wonderful sounds of children laughing when they arrived at the school. With these thoughts in mind, she discarded the traces of apprehension that had crept back into her chest and leaned back as the truck bumped and bounced it's way toward the exit of the compound.

She sat resting against the wooden railings of the truck, letting the warm air rush against her skin. She watched the others become a bit more stiff as the truck left through the secure perimeter of their post. She observed the surrounding village as they drove down the dusty roads and tried to relax, as if she were sightseeing on vacation. She saw rice paddy fields, mountains, and small shanties. Villagers were wearing pointy hats and carrying heavy loads with the help of bamboo braces across their backs. Some were walking, others had rickety old bikes. She took it all in, the sights, the smells, and the sounds. It was so different from what she was used to.

As the truck continued to barrel down the road, Shirley was caught off guard by a rogue bump and accidentally slammed against the boy sitting next to her. She quickly righted herself and apologized. He only smiled and told her it was no problem, took another puff of his cigarette, and exhaled into the sky. Leaning against the railing of the truck, he looked relaxed and approachable, the cig dangling casually between his fingers. Shirley couldn't help but realize how handsome he was, this young medic, smoking and smirking at her. Consequently, their eyes held each other for too long, so they began a conversation to make up for the awkwardness of staring at one another.

"Have you done this before?" Shirley asked him, wondering if she was the only new person on the truck. "This is my first time. What about you?"

He responded with such warmth and invitation that she couldn't help leaning in a little closer, "It's my first time too."

She smiled and tucked her hair behind her ears as the truck bounced onward. She felt more comfortable knowing that they both had no idea what they'd be getting themselves into in just a matter of minutes. They continued to make small talk all the way to the orphanage.

When the truck pulled into the dirt courtyard of the school, any feelings of vulnerability the passengers had been feeling during the ride through town faded away. Orphanages were supposed to be a safe haven during war, and it really felt as though it were. The large truck quickly became surrounded by sweet children calling out in their native tongue and waving to the soldiers. Immediately, Shirley fell in love with the little ones.

Glancing around the compound, her heart became heavy as her mind comprehended what it all meant. This was not just a school, it was an orphanage, and there were so many kids, too many to even count. She thought about how these unfortunate young ones had lost their parents and grandparents and maybe even siblings. She knew that most of them were so young that they had only ever known war. Their entire little lives had been lived during wartime. They were born into families either fighting to be free or trying to live in peace despite the war. Now they were in a group home, and though many of them were too young to be completely devastated by the loss of parents, not fully understanding what it meant to be an orphan, Shirley took the burden on her own heart for them. It was at that moment she truly realized the massive losses that were taking place on both sides of the war. She had been so focused on the American losses while at work, that she didn't really ever think about, much less see, the losses the people of Vietnam were dealing with. There, in the orphanage, she came face to face with their devastation and she was overwhelmed by the sheer number of orphans she was seeing.

Some of these kids had belonged to Vietnamese soldiers and some to simple villagers who were unfortunately caught in the crossfires, as sometimes happens during war. Still, there were others who had just been abandoned by their mothers, leaving their babies at the orphanage gates, knowing they'd be better taken care of by charity than in their own impoverished homes. And still others, who, having been conceived by an American father and a Vietnamese mother (Amerasians), were not accepted anywhere else in Vietnamese culture at that time. The war affected everyone in that land, not just those who were fighting. By the end of the Vietnam war, it was estimated that there were nearly 900,000 orphans left behind (Butterfield, 1975).

To Shirley, many of the kids just looked like typical, healthy kids, but as the blurrs became faces, she noticed that some of the children were also victims of war injuries. Some were amputees, missing legs and hobbling along on old wooden crutches, some were wearing full head wraps, and some were blind, most likely from an explosion. Her heart sank and a knot grew in her throat. How had the war gotten so out of hand? They were just children! She knew that one day, as they grew to understand what had happened to them and their families, they would have a lot of heartache to deal with.

Nevertheless, she looked out at their happy faces with a smile, and loved the sounds of their precious laughter as they entangled themselves with the Americans. After all the trauma they had been through, she thought they showed a resilience that was almost incomprehensible, and she thought it was important to remember that about them. The kids would run up, grab an American's arm and walk around with them. They didn't speak the same language, but it didn't matter to the orphans.

Taking this all in, Shirley decided that the best thing she could do to help them was to love on them and pray for them, and so that's what she did. Climbing down from the truck she was met with freely given hugs, big toothy grins, and lots of tiny bodies wrapping themselves around her arms.

She felt filled in a way she had not expected and was thankful to God that He had given her the courage to leave the compound and come to this place. She looked across the yard and saw the young medic she had been sitting next to on the truck. He was bent down on one knee, children surrounding him on all sides. The kids were climbing on him and laughing, which was infectious, and Shirley saw that he was laughing too. Their eyes met across the yard, and they shared a cherished moment of peace together.

Mike at the Van Coi orphanage in Chu Lai, Vietnam, 1970.

The volunteers were introduced to the nuns and brought in to see the classrooms. Shirley and the young medic were paired together to teach English to the younger learners, kindergarten through third grade. As they stood in front of the class instructing, Shirley knew they were doing the right thing with their time, and she enjoyed every minute of it. After a few hours of playing and English teaching, the volunteers were loaded back onto the truck, chased away by waves, kisses, and shouts of joy from the little ones.

Shirley was glad when the young medic sat down next to her again. She had enjoyed the morning with him, and wanted to get to know him better. They talked about the kids and how much fun they had had. Shirley mentioned that she'd like to do it again next week and was thrilled when the medic said he felt the same way. As the truck thundered down the road, bringing them home, she thought that he was the most genuine person she'd ever met. He seemed so real, right from the start, and she liked that. Realizing that she hadn't even learned his name yet, she said, "Hey, I'm Shirley, by the way." He held his hand out for her to shake and gave it a gentle squeeze, "I'm Mike."

Upon returning to the Army post, Shirley felt exhausted but also hopeful, after having been climbed on by sweet children all day. It was nice to get to interact with them, their innocence so refreshing in the midst of war. She was also feeling exhilarated by meeting that friendly young medic, Mike. He was definitely handsome, but she guessed he was probably a few years younger than she was, an enlisted man and legally off limits, as she was an officer.

Nonetheless, she was happy to have made a new friend. He seemed cool, and he seemed to be genuinely interested in getting to know her. As she made it to her barracks, she laid down for some much needed rest and hoped she'd run into him again before next weekend.

Mike watched Shirley walk all the way back to her barracks and couldn't wipe the smile off his lips. He thought she was wholesome, easy to talk to, unpretentious, and absolutely gorgeous! She knew who she was. He sensed a confidence and a maturity about her that was so attractive, and he hoped he'd get to spend more time with her. He made up his mind right then and there, if she was going to the orphanage every weekend, so was he.

He knew she was a Lieutenant, but that didn't mean they couldn't get to know each other. Besides, in Vietnam, he wasn't too concerned with Army protocol when it came to his personal relationships. They were in the middle of a war and their compound could be bombed any time, any day of the week. He'd worry about dating rules set by the institution another day, if he lived to see one.

In the meantime, his thoughts were fixated on the beautiful woman he'd just met on that truck. He took out a pack of cigarettes, lit up, and felt that familiar calmness overtake him, this time, maybe even mixed with a bit of happiness. A feeling so foreign to him he almost didn't recognize it.

Dawn broke the following Saturday, bringing with it a sense of excitement for their morning. Just as they had planned, Shirley and Mike met at the orphanage truck. Smiling at the sight of one another, they climbed in the back of the vehicle and hoped conversation would come just as easy as it had a week ago.

Mike looked collected and cool and seemed older than his 19 years, cigarette resting between his lips, and maintaining great eye contact as he listened to Shirley speak. Shirley was three years older than he was and normally would think of a boy that much younger than her like a little brother, but with him, there was something about him that seemed so different and she didn't mind the age gap. He was authentic and fresh.

When all of her thoughts about him finally took root, she knew she was in trouble. She hadn't really realized how much she had been looking forward to seeing him again throughout the week, but now that it was happening, she could feel the joy that had been bubbling beneath the surface begin to overflow, and she smiled at him, big and wide. She couldn't deny her attraction to him, and while that seemed innocent enough in her own mind, she knew it'd be a slippery slope if they continued to meet each other every weekend. Oddly enough, she didn't actually care. She liked talking with him, and she wanted to get to know him better, even if it was forbidden for them to date.

Mike loved watching Shirley talk. She was wise and she was smart, the smartest woman he had ever met, and she was always smiling at him. He thought it was nice that someone seemed to genuinely enjoy his company so much. And when she smiled, it was stunning. She had pretty white teeth and soft pink lips and deep brown eyes that matched her hair. He thought he had never laid eyes on anyone so beautiful before.

He continued to ask her all about her life, why she chose to go into nursing, if she liked growing up in Ohio, what she missed about America, and any other questions he could think of, desperately wanting to learn everything he could about her. He loved the way she would always pause for a moment, pondering the question before giving her answers. He had never seen anyone bring so much truth and care to conversation before, and he was becoming addicted to it. It was exhilarating and he consumed her words like the love starved boy he was.

When they reached the orphanage that second time, they were given a little extra tour across the street to see the other orphanage, the Protestant one. Only the Catholic orphanage had a school, but the volunteers were allowed to play with the kids from either orphanage. Right away they began to notice the stark contrast between the two charity groups giving aid to the children. There was a clear distinction between the Catholic side of the orphanage and the Protestant side. To the east, the Catholic church stood tall, strong, and looked clean. The children wore freshly laundered clothing and had actual sheets on their beds. They even had some new toys and were given decent meals. This was not the case for the poor children who had been taken in by the Protestant center.

It was hard for Mike and especially Shirley, being a new Christian, to understand why the other side was so poor. She wondered why the Protestant side had to be so disheveled and hopeless looking. The kids walked around in filthy rags, playing with broken toys and were obviously not as well fed as the little ones from the Catholic side. It was the main reason why Mike and Shirley were attracted to the Protestant side of the orphanage yard during play time. They drew near to the skinny, dirty, little faces who had less—the ones who didn't get meals as often as their bodies asked for them, and who slept on grimy, sheetless mattresses. If Shirley and Mike could bring temporary joy to these orphans, they wanted to spend their time with the ones who seemed to be in the most dire circumstances.

There was one little boy, probably about two years old, that Shirley and Mike fell in love with at first sight. They affectionately called him Ching Chong because they thought he looked like a perfect little China doll. Ching Chong stood out from the rest of the kids because he was always so happy and unlike many of the other kids, he was still fat, plenty of leftover baby chunkiness from his brighter days. His pudgy cheeks and rolly arms stole their hearts in an instant. He was the cutest thing they had seen in that country, and just the sight of him brought them delight.

Ching Chong was too young to understand the hopelessness of his situation, or to think about what might happen to him in the future. He just knew that he liked it when Mike and Shirley would come to visit and he would reward them with adorable smiles and rich baby laughter. From time to time, he'd get tired of playing. and he'd crawl up in one of their laps just wanting to be held. It was so sweet it seemed to tear their hearts into pieces—some of which they never got back.

Left: Shirley holding Ching Chong. Right: Ching Chong at the Van Coi orphanage in Chu Lai, Vietnam.

FORBIDDEN, HIDDEN LOVE

Week after week, Specialist Mike and First Lieutenant Shirley would meet again on the truck to An Tan. Their conversations were natural and sincere, and Mike concluded that Shirley was the most trustworthy person he had ever met. He loved her wavy brown hair, and he thought she looked even more stunning each week, sitting in the back of that truck, clad in OD green head to toe. He wasn't shy about telling her how he felt. He complimented her beauty every chance he got.

Though she was indeed outwardly beautiful, Mike was able to see through to what attracted him to her most, to her inner strength of character. He had never met another human being like Shirley, and he was fascinated by her in every way—her brain, how it worked so efficiently to apply the knowledge she had learned under wartime conditions, how she said she believed in God and then lived that way, her compassion for others, and the way she would look him in the eyes and truly listen while he was talking. There was something different about Shirley that he had not encountered in other young women before. He could imagine a future with her and as they spent more time together, he wondered if he was falling in love.

It wasn't long before Shirley could see that Mike was getting more serious about their relationship. The only problem was that to continue to move toward a romantic relationship with one another would mean to risk getting court marshalled by the Army. Usually Shirley was all about following the rules. She knew it was important to keep protocols and thought of herself as a good, law-abiding officer. But when it came to Mike, her feelings for him were stronger than her desire to live by the rules. Besides, she rationalized, she would never be his commanding officer, and that's what the rule was really about anyway. She had heard people say that some rules were meant to be broken, and now she finally understood what they meant. From that moment on, she fully intended to let her heart slip away, piece by piece, she'd give it to Mike until she had nothing left. She prayed he felt the same way.

Shirley and Mike began spending all of their free time together. As the weeks went by, their effort to hide their newfound love faded. They became lazy with hiding their intentions, and though none of their physical behavior could be used to indict them because they didn't hold hands, kiss, or show any affection in public, the way they looked at each other and their constant proximity to one another was enough to know there was something special going on between the two.

FORBIDDEN, HIDDEN LOVE

Left: Shirley holding a child at the orphanage. Center: Falling in love. Right: Mike taking a smoke break outside the OR.

Mike and Shirley would get off from their 12-hour shifts, they'd walk to the edge of the coast, sit on the rocks, and watch the choppers come in. It was over many nights like these, that they really gave themselves to each other. They'd ask more questions, make more jokes, share more stories from their pasts and dreams for their futures. It was a night like this, when Hueys were descending overhead, that they rested their foreheads together with their eyes closed, breathing each other's air, enjoying the closeness and the peace together.

Mike had been wanting to kiss her for so long and there, in the middle of the night, sitting on those rocky cliffs with the sounds of choppers and bombing in the distance, he did it. He pressed his lips to hers and at that moment, they both knew how serious their relationship had become.

Shirley and Mike became even more bold as a couple by sitting on the enlisted side of the cafeteria together. She was an officer, of course, and was supposed to eat on the officer side, but decided she'd rather spend what may be her last meal eating next to the boy from Florida, the enlisted boy who was three years younger than she was, and who smoked cigarettes. The handsome man she first saw on the truck to An Tan and who loved Ching Chong as much as she did. That's who she would eat her meals with, and no one was going to stop her.

Slowly, as friends and coworkers began to pick up on their secret relationship, Mike and Shirley collected a rather large fanbase around the post. With support from fellow officers and enlisted alike, they became even more bold and sometimes Mike would actually eat on the officer side of the cafeteria with Shirley or join her in the Officers' Club! This was utterly unacceptable. But there, in Vietnam, people smiled to themselves and winked at the happy couple to show their support. They took pleasure in knowing that something good was coming out of it all. Something beautiful, like love, was present in their lives and they could all hope for it to succeed. The fact that their relationship was in blatant opposition to the rules of the Army was just a bonus that made Mike and Shirley even more popular and well-liked around the post. Their relationship was seen as somewhat of a peaceful rebellion against the institution, and they became a symbol of hope in Chu Lai, receiving silent applause and cheering from their comrades everywhere they went together.

On their way to the Officers' Club.

The United States Military took fraternizing very seriously . . . stateside. Fortunately, for Mike and Shirley, there wasn't much that could be done to stop them in the middle of a war, halfway around the world. Their relationship was completely illegal and would not for a moment have been tolerated in the States. Shirley and Mike had become an official couple, and they were falling madly in love with one another. They both knew they loved each other, but saying it out loud felt like they might jinx the whole thing.

It happened so fast, the bonding. In the matter of a few short months, they had gone all in. They had held nothing back, and amidst the daily heartache, they clung to each other. They survived by dreaming big dreams of a life they could create together back in the world. Mike and Shirley had become inseparable, bound by a mutual love for the orphans of the war, and a hope for a better and more peaceful future than either of them had ever known. In their minds, they'd be together forever. And though they knew how they felt, they both believed there would be a right time to say it, and when that time came, they'd know it.

No longer hiding their affection for one another.

At one point, as their relationship became more obvious to the higher ups, Mike and Shirley were told to report to the commanding officer of the hospital. They sat side by side, staring at the man across the room, a weighty desk between them. It all had an air of formality and they were asked very directly if the two of them were involved in a relationship with each other—a relationship that would be breaking Army law and would have to be ended immediately. The officer could tell by their lack of enthusiastic denial that there was something more going on between the two, and gave them a harsh warning to stay away from each other. In response to the rigid warning from the CO, Mike jokingly asked, "What are you gonna do? Send me to Vietnam?" The CO shook his head at the disrespect and gestured for them to leave. With that, they returned to their barracks unfazed.

One day these young men and women of the Army were alive, the next day they weren't. What rules could the Army really enforce in that type of environment? New boots quickly found out that things in Vietnam ran a little more informally than back in the States. Unfortunately, for officers who tried to enforce stateside rules too heavily, some of them ended up KIA, fragged by their own men.

Stateside rules that are taught in a peacetime environment do not work in a foreign land during a wartime. For an officer to demand that a soldier shower, shave, and put on clean clothes before he or she can have some food, when that soldier just walked onto the post hungry, having spent a month in the bush killing people and watching friends die in barbaric ways and will only going to have one night of peace before returning to the fighting is unreasonable and unfathomable. It didn't stop certain leaders from making these kinds of demands, trying to enforce the Army code above the Human code. It just didn't work.

When young kids, drafted into war, do not expect to live past the next 12 months, there isn't much they won't do to make their last days as enjoyable as environmentally possible. Whether that means fragging their self-righteous leaders, escaping reality with drugs, or fraternizing with members of the opposite sex, there isn't much that can be done to stop the people who believe they are going to die soon. For Mike and Shirley, that meant falling in love. Even if it was against the rules.

On Thanksgiving Day 1970, Shirley was celebrating with the other officers who had the day off by playing a leisurely game of beach volleyball and forgetting the war with round after round of beer. Being a conservative young woman and an outspoken Christian, Shirley had not had much experience with alcohol in her young life and didn't realize how much she was drinking. By noon, the young Lieutenant was having too much fun for her own good. Fellow officers took her to the hospital where Mike was working and told her to wait outside. They promptly went in to find Mike and tell him that he needed to go take care of Shirley, that she'd had too much to drink. Out of all the people on the post, including Barb, he was the one they came to get, and that's when he knew their relationship was officially recognized by others. That's when he knew it was real.

A friend covered the rest of his shift so he could go care for Shirley. When he came out to meet her, what he found was a very happy and overly relaxed Lieutenant. He had never seen her like this, and he smiled as he walked toward her, happy to be the one to deal with the aftermath of her drinking inexperience. He knew he had to get her out of the hospital area before she was seen in such a condition by their superiors.

Mike helped her stand and offered her much needed stability as they stumbled together back toward the barracks. He placed a cold washcloth on her forehead, told her she would feel better soon and waited with her until she fell asleep. As he watched her sleep, her eyelids fluttering with dreams and her breathing slow and rhythmic, he realized that taking care of her like this was something he wanted to do forever. He wanted to be the one by her side until they were gray and old. It was then that he wanted to tell her he loved her. She slept on, and he smiled to himself thinking about their future and about how he might deliver those sacred words to her.

As the holiday season came into full swing around the post, Shirley knew she had some tough news to break to Mike, and she prayed that he wouldn't change his mind about her. She had not expected their relationship to evolve the way it did so quickly and had never found the right time to mention that there was a man back home who was in her life. To be honest, many times when she was with Mike throughout the past couple of months, she had completely forgotten about the guy she was dating back home. As her first R&R was quickly approaching, she knew she must tell him about Darrell. In just a couple of weeks she'd be going to Hawaii, and according to the plan they had made before Shirley left for Vietnam, Darrell was going to be meeting her there.

Shirley had stopped sending letters to Darrell as soon as she knew the way she felt about Mike, but she hadn't told either of them about the other yet, which she fully intended to do. She just didn't know how or when to do it. She had never been in such a situation, and her heart ached thinking about the potential pain she may cause to one or both of them.

As the days neared for her departure to Hawaii, she knew she must tell Mike. She had come up with a plan in her mind, and it was brilliant. She'd skip her R&R! She'd choose to stay in Vietnam with Mike and that would show him how serious she was about him. As for Darrell, she'd write him a letter and apologize for not showing up in Hawaii. She'd tell him the truth and hope he would forgive her. But the reality was, she didn't love Darrell, she loved Mike and it was never more clear to her than in the past couple of weeks thinking about Hawaii.

Apprehensive about the conversation, she went to Mike to clear her conscience and to remove all hindrances from a future romance with one another. She waited for him to get off his shift and invited him to her barracks for dinner. Sometimes they'd make spaghetti on the small electric hot plate she had, and they'd have a private meal, a nice change from the mess hall. Not knowing exactly where to begin, but feeling confident in her plan, she spilled it all out. She told him that she and Darrell had sort of been dating back in the States, and that they'd written to each other, but that she hadn't written to him in months, since she met Mike and started to have such strong feelings for him. She told him that she didn't love Darrell and thought of the relationship they had as just a comfort of having someone back home who cared about her. Finally, she told him that she didn't have to go to Hawaii if he didn't want her to. All he had to do was ask, and she'd stay.

Mike took it all in slowly. He didn't say much at first, but he was completely crushed. His heart ached in a way he had never felt and dreams of a future with Shirley, this amazing woman, came to a sudden and severe halt. He should've known. She was too awesome to not have anyone waiting on her back home. Why hadn't he asked her about past relationships before? Before he let his heart go?

Immediately he felt the old familiar walls start to rise. His tried and true protection, more solid than his hard helmet and more secure than the Chu Lai perimeter. His appetite was gone, and he told Shirley he wanted to be left alone. With that, he stood and held her eyes with his own for a moment in silence before exiting her barracks.

Shirley didn't know what had just happened. She knew he wouldn't like that there was someone else, but she thought she had offered good news along with it. She thought she had heavily implied that she would stay in Vietnam and skip Hawaii if that's what he wanted. She wondered if perhaps she hadn't been clear. The words had all spilled out and she wasn't exactly sure what she had actually said and what she had implied. Though she was confused about his reaction, she figured the best thing to do was to give him the space he had asked for and pray about it. Surely in the morning he would be calmed down and everything would be back to normal between the two of them.

When she saw him the next morning, he was more rigid and less familiar than the Mike she knew. He was calm, but distant, and it hurt them both. He could tell that she wanted him to ask her not to go to Hawaii. He wanted to ask her to stay, but it didn't seem right. If she wanted to stay, she'd have to make that decision on her own, he was not going to ask her to stay.

He had no idea who Darrell was or what they had going on back home. So instead of asking her to stay with him, he told her that she should go to Hawaii. She had to go and see Darrell and know for sure the way she felt. He didn't want her to make the biggest decision of her life based on a couple of months of a relationship they had built in the midst of war. Their relationship would be on hold until she got back.

It really bothered Shirley that Mike hadn't asked her to stay, and it confused her. Had she misread the way he felt about her? Mike was also upset that Shirley hadn't chosen on her own to stay. He had a tiny sliver of hope that she'd decide not to go to Hawaii, and they'd stay together and build a future together. They were both waiting on the other one to reveal their true feelings and in the week leading up to her departure their relationship had cooled way down.

The morning came for Shirley's flight to Honolulu, and she was surprised to find that Mike was not awake. He had given her a letter the night before, enclosed in an envelope that read, "Open when you are among the clouds and racing with the birds."

She carried the envelope in her hands, waiting for the moment when she could tear into it. She loved the way Mike always wrote poetically. In their brief relationship so far, he had written her several love letters and left little notes for her to find. Sometimes he'd copy one of his favorite poems for her into his own handwriting. He was so romantic that way and she adored it.

The letter Mike gave Shirley to read on her way to Hawaii.

Disappointed that he had not gotten up to say goodbye, she went to the OR to see if he was sleeping there, like he sometimes did. Her heart was beating so fast, and she hoped and prayed that he'd see her and change his mind—that he'd tell her not to go, to just stay there with him. And she would. She'd drop her bags, and she'd stay without a second thought. Unfortunately, that's not what happened. She woke him up, and he barely acted alive. Nonchalantly, casually, half asleep, he told her goodbye. No hug, no kiss, he didn't even get out of bed! It just about killed her on the inside. Him too. But she knew his walls had come up and the only way to break them back down was to go to Hawaii and break things off with Darrell.

As the plane reached altitude, Shirley ripped open the envelope and devoured his words as quickly as she could.
Then she reread them slower, pondering each sentence carefully for meaning. Mike had written her a love poem by

FORBIDDEN, HIDDEN LOVE

Leonard Cohen. The words were recorded beautifully in Mike's own handwriting, the emerald green ink stared up at Shirley, reminding her of his hazel green eyes. On the third and final page, he wrote three lines of his own.

> Now I wait
> God bless and keep you
> until then

He signed his name at the bottom. Shirley read it over and over, encouraged that he'd be waiting for her when she got back. She wished her trip didn't have to be so long. A full week without talking to him would be miserable. As the plane soared on, Shirley decided to share her story with her seatmate to see what he thought about it all. Did he think Mike would really wait for her? Did he think Darrell would be angry? Was she making the right choice? Throughout the rest of the flight, she inundated him with her problems, and more than getting any advice, she just needed someone to listen to her. Someone who was not involved in the situation to hear it from her perspective. The guy barely got two words in, and she felt bad about it afterward, but it did seem to help her work through some of her thoughts.

Darrell was waiting for her when she disembarked from the plane. Just as they had planned months ago, he was there, and he was holding a bouquet of flowers. This was not going to be as easy as she had imagined. He wore a big smile, genuinely happy to see her, and together they made their way to the hotel. She felt so terrible inside she thought she might get sick. Darrell was such a sweet guy. He was reliable, and they had spent all that time in training together. She knew he was not the one for her, but he sure was loyal and she appreciated that about him. She didn't want to have to do this, but she knew her heart belonged to someone else. Darrell seemed to sense that she was not feeling well, and she asked him if they could go for a walk along the beach somewhere. The sooner she got it over with, the better, she thought.

They found a place to sit on the edge of the ocean, a nice seawall along Waikiki beach. It was fairly private, as good a place as any to have this dreadful conversation. Before she could start with her story though, he pulled a diamond ring out of his pocket, held it out to her and asked her to marry him!

Shirley gasped, completely shocked by the unexpected proposal. They hadn't even been that close; how could this be happening? So many thoughts came rushing through her mind and she didn't want to tell him no. That seemed too harsh for some reason, so she told him that she didn't know. Which wasn't true, she did know that she couldn't marry him because she didn't love him. Darrell started asking her questions, tons of questions about why she wouldn't marry him. He was hurt and angry and wanted to know if there was another guy.

As she unveiled her story before him, she could see the air physically leaving his lungs. He looked deflated and defeated, and he kept shaking his head. When Shirley tried to encourage him that this was the right thing to do, that they weren't really in love, he took the engagement ring in his hand and threatened to throw it in the ocean. She felt terrible as knots turned in her stomach, and she made herself think of Mike. Of her future with him, their future children, and their future home. She needed the strength of those happy thoughts to continue to break Darrell's heart, as much as she hated herself in the moment for doing it.

Darrell went through the full spectrum of emotions right there on that beach. Thankfully, she convinced him not to throw the ring in the ocean. She knew he'd spent a lot of money on it, and when he calmed down, he could return it, or sell it. They sat there awhile with him asking questions about Mike, and Shirley trying to answer them respectfully. She figured she at least owed him the truth. He had come all that way. He eventually calmed down, realizing there was nothing he could do to change the situation. They walked back to the hotel and tried to talk about other things.

The week went on and they spent time together talking things out. They visited Pearl Harbor and did some of the touristy things. It was a bit awkward but she got through it and by the end of the R&R, they were on good terms.

Darrell realized that maybe Shirley was right. Maybe they didn't really love each other. Maybe he had just been in love with the idea of having a committed relationship. They liked each other, but it wasn't true love. At the end of the week, he took her back to the airport, and they said goodbye for the last time.

When she got back on the plane, her mind was focused on one thing. Getting back to Mike. She missed him so much and started counting down the hours. They had dealt with the biggest hurdle and now the future was a blank canvas for them. She only hoped he was really waiting for her to get back and wouldn't have changed his mind in her absence.

While Shirley was off in Hawaii, Mike became restless. He couldn't just sit around waiting for her to reject him. For her to see Darrell and remember how much she loved him and come back and break his heart. No. He couldn't stay still waiting for that to happen. As much as he hoped for her to come back and still want him, he made himself start moving on. He wanted to have a head start if things didn't work out the way he hoped. His 19-year-old ego couldn't handle it any other way. So he forced himself to attend the after work parties and talk to other nurses.

One nurse in particular seemed to like him, and she was nice enough. He told her his sad story of how Shirley had left to meet another guy on her R&R, and he didn't know what would happen when she got back. She felt sorry for him, the way he had hoped she would, and they began hanging out. Her name was Mayge and she was quite beautiful. Mike thought she was pretty, but she didn't even come close to Shirley's beauty in his mind. His heart belonged to Shirley now, and he knew there was nothing he could do to get it back. If he would be crushed on the inside, he'd at least look fine to everyone else on the outside, he promised himself that. With those thoughts in mind, he spent much of his time with Mayge while Shirley was gone.

When Shirley got off the plane, the first thing someone said to her was that she shouldn't think Mike had been waiting around for her to get back. She quickly learned about his hanging around with Mayge and went straight to find him. Fortunately for them both, absence had indeed made their hearts grow fonder, and relief flooded their faces as their eyes met.

Mike held Shirley in his arms and made a mental promise to himself to never let her go again. She had come back to him. She had broken things off with Darrell. She told him it was so good to be back and that she had missed him so much, and it made him feel light and free. Mayge would have to find a new friend, because he was now off the market for good!

Around this time, many soldiers were preparing to spend their first Christmas at war. Shirley was doing her job as usual, stitching up wounds, applying bandages, and saying prayers for the soldiers, asking God to let them survive so they could make it home to their families one day. She spent some time on her day off hanging what little decorations they had leftover from soldiers who had spent Christmas in Vietnam the previous years. Across the base, people had been doing similar things and it actually did seem to make the place a little more cheery.

One night, Mike came over to hang ornaments from a fresh care package Shirley had received from home. They were feeling good, getting into the holiday spirit, and they began daydreaming about their futures. Daydreaming aloud together quickly became a favorite pastime and in a matter of weeks, they had planned out years of their lives together. Fantasies about traveling the country, building their own house on some land in a quiet town and raising children together. They didn't know any of the details, but they fell in love with what could be in store for them when they'd get to leave the war behind and build a new life together. A life of peace together.

As they pulled more ornaments out of the box, Shirley noticed that one of them was a small, pale blue baby rattle. She had asked her mom a couple of months back to send some new toys in the next care package for the kids at the orphanage. Her mom packed the box full of toys and knowing it would arrive around the holidays, she had included some Christmas ornaments too, among them, this rattle. Undoubtedly her mom had been thinking that a baby might like to play with it, but something about it struck Shirley. She carefully hung the little ornament on her tree and it brought her so much unexpected joy every time she saw it. It made her think that one day, she and Mike would have a baby together. And then they'd hang that rattle on their family Christmas tree.

The blue rattle ornament Shirley saved from her first Christmas with Mike in Vietnam. It has graced the Hensley family Christmas tree every year since 1970.

When it came time to take the ornaments down and give them away as toys to the orphans, Shirley made sure to tuck that little blue rattle away into a safe place. It was going to be theirs, forever. A small symbol of their young love and their hope for a bright future. Christmas came and went and was pretty much just like all of the other days at war. It was hard on a lot of people who had never been away from their families for the holidays. But they banded together and celebrated as best as they could with music, drinks, and dancing.

On the weekend after Christmas, they went to the orphanage, bringing the toys with them to hand out as presents for the kids to share. Shirley had also brought a special Christmas present just for Ching Chong. It was a flowered Hawaiian shirt and shorts set that she had picked up in a gift shop in Honolulu. He put on that fresh shirt, blue with white and yellow hibiscus flowers, and strutted around the orphanage yard like he owned the place. Chin up, chest puffed out, standing tall and proud of his new outfit, marching around to make sure all of the other kids could see him. It just about broke Shirley's heart. At one point she even wondered about adopting Ching Chong, but being so young and unmarried, not to mention in a foreign country that was at war with itself, she just didn't even know where to start. But she loved him, and she knew she'd always remember him. Always.

As Christmas came and went, Mike and Shirley continued to work feverishly to save the lives of American soldiers. War didn't stop for nights, weekends, or holidays, and guys proceeded to come in from the dust offs clinging to life, desperately in need of a savior. Shirley prayed as she worked on the less intensive patients, talking with them and making sure they were well taken care of. Many of them worried that their wives and girlfriends back home wouldn't be able to handle their injuries, that they were too ugly, too maimed, or had too many missing body parts and altered features to have a good future. They were hopeless.

Shirley always tried to reassure them that their loved ones would be so thankful they were alive. That they'd see past the injuries, that there was hope for their lives to still be good in spite of the misfortune they had suffered. It was emotionally grueling. She hurt so bad for them, especially the youngest ones. Only eighteen years old and facing the rest of their lives with no legs . . . or arms . . . or a mangled face . . . depending on what horror had visited them in the bush. It was absolutely heartbreaking. And these were the ones that were going to live.

When a new batch of trauma patients would come in, young guys freshly blown to pieces, but somehow still breathing, she would automatically go into life-saving mode, whatever it took and was in her power to do, she did it. She was well educated in her craft, efficient, accurate, and fantastic at knowing exactly what a patient needed and how to perform the task with great precision. Her brain and body connected like a well-oiled machine in those moments, and she would move quickly into action, effectively playing her part in saving the lives of those unfortunate young men.

Mike was no different. He was a top rated medic, highly sought by each of the surgeons in the 91st evacuation hospital. Mike not only learned, and to great mastery, each of the skills he needed to be a life saving force in the war, but he quickly and fluently learned each of the doctors he worked with. He learned their methods, their preferred tools, and surgical styles. He understood the operations so well, and the doctors performing them, that he almost always knew what tool they needed before they even asked for it, and would have it ready to hand them. The doctors loved working with Mike, this being one of the main reasons. He was incredibly smart, and not afraid to take over certain operations to free up the doctors to move on to the next patient. He became so trusted by the doctors that they would often perform the necessary surgery and then leave Mike to do the stitching back up on his own.

The two young lovers spent their days and nights leading up to the new year working their shifts together and then spending their time off together. They always wanted to be near one another and when they were working in their separate units at work, they would still make eye contact from across the room and smile at one another as they passed patients back and forth between the ICU/Recovery quonset hut (where Shirley worked) and the OR/Surgical quonset hut (Where Mike worked). These two quonset buildings were connected by a hallway and almost all of Mike's patients ended up in recovery with

Shirley. This meant they got to see each other multiple times during their 12-hour shifts and just a simple smile from across the room gave them each the energy they needed to keep going strong until the end of their shifts.

When they weren't working together and the alarm would sound for a possible incoming rocket, they would run to their underground bunkers, and Mike would always run to whichever bunker Shirley was in. It didn't matter if he had to run past a closer bunker on his way there; if he was going to die over there, he was going to do it next to Shirley. Others began to notice that Mike kept showing up in the nurses' bunker every time that alarm screamed in the middle of the night, but no one said anything, they always just smiled and passed the time with small talk and speculations about how long they'd be down there.

As the new year came upon them, Shirley and Mike attended a New Year's Eve party at the Officers' Club. He thought this would be the perfect opportunity to tell her how he really felt about her. They were celebrating, they were in their civilian clothes, and they were starting a brand new year, the one in which they'd return to America, and if all went according to their plans, get married! It was definitely the night to tell her that he loved her and he was giddy with the anticipation of speaking those holy words to this woman.

As the minutes were closing in on midnight, Mike asked Shirley to dance with him. The music was playing loud, the air was warm, and people all around them were having fun, dancing, laughing, and smiling. He pulled her in close, holding her in his arms, and swaying to the music. They were surrounded by people but had all the privacy of their own little world and as they danced and as the time ticked away the year, he whispered the words in her ear.

Chapter Seven

WE GOTTA GET OUT OF THIS PLACE

Mike and Shirley were working the same shift at the 91st Evacuation hospital in Chu Lai, when the doors at the end of the ward flung open wide and stretchers with newly dying boys came rushing down the hall. One particular young man came in screaming in pure agony, somehow still awake in his pain and Shirley noticed how his flesh was dripping off of his bones, landing in liquid-like pools on the edge of his stretcher. Immediately the smell polluted the air in the ward ... the terrible, unforgettable, and unmistakable stench of burnt flesh. Shirley collected her thoughts and told herself to ignore the smell and just do her job as she helped guide his stretcher into place, where they promptly began to medicate him.

Over the next few days, Shirley would come into the ICU ward, where the burn victim was being treated, and get to work. She'd carefully remove his blood soaked bandages and replace them with fresh ones. She thought it was the toughest job she'd ever done. She knew how unbelievably bad the pain was from a burn, and this young man had been badly burnt over 95 percent of his body. Almost all of his skin was gone, and she knew he was not going to make it. People cannot live when that much of their skin is missing. It broke her heart to know that he wouldn't make it home. Here he was, alive, and there was nothing anyone could do to save him. The only thing they could do was medicate him to ease the pain until he finally passed on to the next life.

Shirley saw him as just a child, and she wanted him to know that she was there with him, that she'd be there whenever he needed her. Mike had met the young boy too, and they both tried to offer him dignity in his dying days by talking with him and spending time with him. Though in much pain and on much medication, he was coherent.

During one particular conversation, just a few days after the young soldier had come into their care wailing in agony, he made a simple request of his new friend. He had come to realize that his condition was too great to heal, that he would not get to go home. He said he knew that he was dying, and it wouldn't be long before he was gone—and he had one last wish, a final word in the world he would be leaving too soon. He asked Shirley if she would write to his folks back home and tell them that he was okay. That he missed them and loved them and that he died comfortably in his bed, knowing that it was coming and being okay with it. He wanted them to have that gift. The gift of knowing how he died and that he wasn't afraid. He may have lied about the part that he was comfortable in the end, but that would be his and Shirley's secret. He wanted his family to be okay, and he believed that if Shirley wrote to them, it would make a big difference.

Her heart stung as if it'd just been injected with poison. This was too much to bear. As her eyes filled with tears, she shook her head. He asked her to promise that she would do it, promise him that she wouldn't forget. She promised. With his final wish secured, he closed his eyes one last time, and he was gone. She sat there for a moment, a new kind of sober washing over her. She thought about his mother and father, his siblings and friends, how at that exact moment, their baby, their brother, their friend had left this world for good, and they had no idea. What were they doing back in the world? How long would it take for the Army to let them know he had been killed?

Glancing around the ward, through glassy eyes, everything looked different. She hated this place. More than that, she loathed it. She loathed the war and what it was doing to young American boys, she detested the barbaric booby traps the enemy set up to torture them and she hated the draft . . . knowing that many of these boys didn't even sign up for this, that their government had owned them like property and made them go into those brutal bush fights where they were not only killed but mutilated . . . that made it even worse. She wondered what the young burn victim, now eternally departed from the world, had wanted to do with his life. What dreams did he have when he was a little boy, not so long ago? What had he wanted to become before his government stole his life and gave it away? She hadn't asked him. It seemed wrong to ask that question of a dying man knowing he'd never get to become it, whatever it was. But she wished she knew.

She made it through the rest of her shift detached from reality. Going through the motions, changing bandages, and smiling at healing soldiers and offering them an encouraging word, but her mind was with the burn victim. She thought it was strange that no death thus far had affected her like this, but then again, most of the boys that died didn't ask her to write home to their families. In fact, he was the only one who had ever asked her to do that.

When her shift was over, she went and found Mike. She had to talk about it; she needed to let him know that the kid had died, and that he'd made her promise to write to his folks. Mike could tell that Shirley was a wreck on the inside, and his heart ached for the soldier too. He held her in his arms, stroked her soft hair, and then told her she'd better go write that letter. A promise is a promise, he told her, and she had to do it. The sooner she got it over with, the better.

Shirley left for her barracks, the boy's family address crumpled up in a piece of paper in her hand. She dug out her box of stationery and a pen and sat frozen at her desk for a while, just thinking. She wanted to imagine being the recipient of her letter. She wanted it to be as least painful as possible for them to read, but she wasn't sure how to do that. No matter what she wrote, it was going to hurt them. She decided to keep it short, just his words and a few condolences of her own. After about an hour, she had it done, brought it to the mailroom, and placed it with the outgoing mail.

She stared at the envelope there for a moment, stacked on top of all the others that would be heading home soon. She thought most of them were probably simple updates and requests for specific items in their next care packages . . . but not hers. When hers was delivered, that boys' family would break down in tears again. They'd face his death again, and they'd miss him, and they'd cry, and they'd be reminded that they were never going to see him again. She gave her envelope one last look, swallowed the knot in her throat, and then walked back to her barracks.

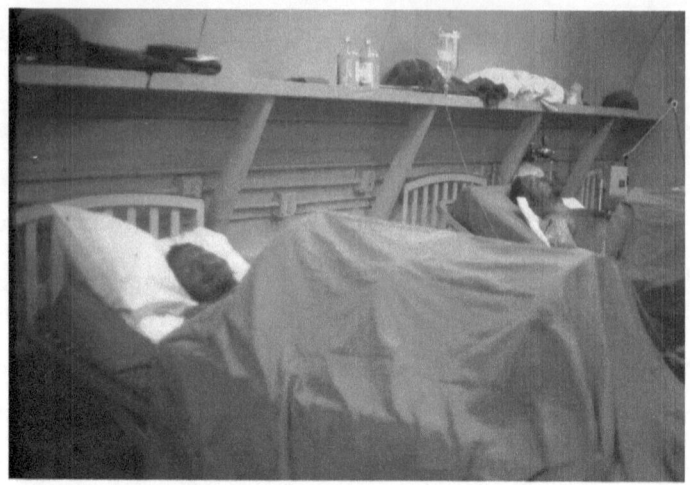

The burn victim who sent his final words to his family through Shirley's promise.

As the days at war continued on, Mike was getting more and more used to operating on enemy soldiers. The doctors knew him well by now and trusted him even more to do simple operations on VC and NVA when they were busy working on Americans. Mike despised the enemy soldiers, and the way he thought of them became increasingly less humane. They were dogs, they were dirt, they were nothing. It got to the point where he was so upset about seeing his brothers come in torn to pieces, that he even disliked Vietnamese civilians. He couldn't stand anything about the place. The heat, the smell, and especially the people! He had so much anger from seeing all the dying around him every day, and it had to be directed somewhere, so why not the entire country? Everyone except the orphans.

As he was preparing an enemy soldier for surgery one day, removing the man's jacket to access the injury, a photograph fell out of the chest pocket. Mike picked it up off the floor, turned it over and was surprised to see a beautiful young woman and a child in the photo. He examined the picture for quite awhile, concluding that the woman must be his wife and the toddler their child. He looked back down at the man he was about to operate on, and it was weird, but he didn't hate him anymore.

He didn't particularly like him, far from it, but he didn't hate him either. That photo, those people in it, he couldn't get it out of his mind. He wondered if this young man had chosen to fight or if the North Vietnamese communists had made his choice for him. He guessed the latter and with that, he felt sorry for the man, just as he felt sorry for the Americans who had been selected for war by the draft.

For the first time ever, he thought maybe the enemy was the same as him in some ways. Maybe they didn't want to be fighting either, maybe they'd rather be at home, at peace with their families, and maybe they were just doing what they were told by their leaders. Kill the Americans. Isn't that what the Americans had been told? Kill the enemy. Of course, there were reasons behind all the killing that men in conference rooms far away from the war were coming up with. But as far as Mike could see, when it all boiled down to the basics, they were there to kill the enemy. To stop them. To stop the spread of communism.

On the ground, to the grunts in the bush, it didn't matter why. It only mattered that they killed the enemy before the enemy killed them. That was it. And in that way, Mike could finally see that both sides were more similar than he had first thought. That photograph really opened his eyes. He started to feel less hate for the enemy soldiers. He still didn't really care if they died of their injuries, but it didn't make him glad anymore, because he now had a better understanding of the humanness of war.

As the war continued and the days ticked away, Mike and Shirley realized that soon it would be Valentine's day, their first one together! They decided that when their shifts were over, they'd meet at the commissary, which was like the neighborhood grocery store for their base, and then head back to Shirley's barracks for a special dinner at home.

Shirley would use the hot plate and a large wok to boil spaghetti noodles and they'd pour a jar of tomato sauce over top. It was surprisingly delicious, and it was one of their favorite meals together. The hot plate had to be plugged into the floor of Shirley's barracks because that's where the outlet was and the cord wasn't long enough to set it up on the counter. So, Shirley would crouch down around the boiling water, stirring the noodles and preparing their special meals. They would forgo the mess hall about once every two weeks to eat in the barracks instead.

Their Valentine's day plans were set, and they were both looking forward to celebrating their young love. But on February 13, Mike came down with a pretty high fever and was having a lot of pain in his abdomen. After some quick assessments, it was decided that Mike was suffering from appendicitis and would need to undergo emergency surgery right away! One of the doctors Mike and Shirley both knew would be the one to perform the operation.

When Shirley heard the news, she was worried for Mike and felt terrible that he was in such pain, but she trusted that doctor, as he was the best. Mike was put under general anesthesia and the appendectomy was underway. Shirley stayed at the hospital waiting and praying that the surgery would be successful and Mike would recover quickly.

When it was finished, Mike was wheeled into the recovery room. The surgery had been a success and though he had just had his abdomen sliced open, he was already feeling much better.

The next day, instead of having a romantic night in, making dinner and celebrating their first Valentine's day together, Shirley spent the day taking care of Mike as he recovered from the procedure. Mike felt so bad about ruining their first romantic holiday that he looked around his hospital bed for something he could use to make her a card. He found a discarded scrap of cardboard nearby. The front was printed on, but the back was blank! He found a pair of scissors and cut the cardboard into the shape of a heart and wrote a simple but meaningful message to Shirley on it. "To my very own Valentine (forever). I'm a downer, but I love you. Michael."

He thought it was perfect! It said everything. He was committed to her for the rest of his life, that was the (forever) part, that he was sorry for ruining their first Valentine's day by getting sick (I'm a downer), and that he loved her! They had only just begun saying those words to each other and it was nice to write them down for her.

He thought she would love it and he felt good about finding the supplies just lying around. He even thought the shape of his heart was pretty darn good also. He was actually looking forward to giving it to her when she came back.

WE GOTTA GET OUT OF THIS PLACE

Mike (showing off his appendectomy scar) and Shirley celebrating their first Valentine's Day a week late on the cliffs of the South China Sea.
Top Right: Mike's homemade Valentine's Day card from his hospital room.

When Shirley walked into Mike's recovery room with dinner, he surprised her with the cardboard heart, and he was right. She loved it! She read the short, sweet message and beamed, knowing he took the time to craft together a gift for her, and that he said "forever" when addressing her as his very own Valentine.

That's one of the things he loved most about her. She didn't have certain expectations of him. She didn't require flowers and jewelry and dancing and real cards and expensive gestures of his love. She was happy with whatever he gave, even if it was a quickly scribbled note on the back of an envelope or a napkin, expressing his love for her.

He was so thankful for her personality, for her gratefulness and genuine happiness at whatever he was able to do for her, that he made up his mind right then and there. If he ever made decent money one day and had extra, he would shower her with gifts and adorn her in jewels, because she was the kind of woman who deserved it and because she didn't demand it.

He watched her hold the little cardboard heart close to her chest, like a treasure, smiling at him with those warm brown eyes and soft pink lips. After dinner she kissed him goodnight, wishing him a happy Valentine's day and whispering in his ear that it was the best one she'd ever had. He went to sleep feeling more in love than he had the day before.

Shirley made it to her room and read his words on the little cardboard heart one more time, smiling to herself as she closed her eyes to sleep. She was thrilled to have received her first Valentine's card from the first man she had ever truly loved. She believed him when he said forever, and she prayed that forever would last a long time for them.

About a month later, Mike was well recovered from surgery and found himself getting on a plane. He was leaving for his R&R to Australia. Shirley wrote to him every day, even though she'd only be able to hand the letters to him when he got back. She felt more lonely than she had felt in a very long time with him being gone. They had just taken their relationship to the next level by talking about marriage and dreaming out loud about their futures together. They openly and easily said that they loved each other, shared all of their emotions with one another, and were both all in when it came to talking about forever together.

She hoped that being away from her, around a bunch of blonde beauties in the land down under, wouldn't make him change his mind about her. She knew he loved her, and she believed him when he said he wanted to spend forever with her, but there was still a part of her that felt insecure. Still a piece of her past self that told her she wasn't good enough, that it was just the war that was making them so close and that when he got out, and was around other women, maybe he'd realize that she was a big mistake.

She kept telling herself not to think like that, and she comforted her anxieties by turning these disconcerting thoughts all over to God in prayer. She trusted that whatever was meant to be, would be. After all of that negative thinking was settled, all she could do was wait and pray that he'd come back and still be excited about making a life with her.

Though Mike would miss Shirley while he was gone, he was really looking forward to his time away. He had made up his mind that while he was in Australia he would find and buy an engagement ring for Shirley. As he thought about a lifelong commitment to the beautiful, amazing First Lieutenant, he knew that she would be his one and only woman, forever. He thought about his parents, how they had gotten divorced and his mom remarried. He thought about love, trust, and honesty, all the things he imagined would add up to a successful marriage, and he wholeheartedly believed that Shirley had everything he'd ever want or need.

How had his greatest misfortune, being sent to Vietnam, turned into his luckiest break, meeting the perfect woman? He thought it was almost too good to be true. And at that thought, he said a quick prayer that they'd both survive the rest of their days at war, and he hoped Shirley's God was listening.

He spent his days going in and out of different jewelry shops in Sydney. It was more difficult than he thought it was going to be. He was only 19 years old and had enlisted in the army 10 days after graduating from high school. He didn't have a ton of money saved up but wanted to get her something really nice, something that would show her how serious he was, that he loved her, and wanted to spend the rest of his life with her. He didn't put a lot of pressure on finding a ring right away.

He made sure to enjoy his time in a peaceful land, a land where he spoke the same language and felt safe. He was staying with an Australian family who had volunteered to host American soldiers who were on R&R. At that time, they were hosting Mike and another guy from the Army that Mike hadn't met before. He liked the guy and liked the family but spent a lot of his time alone, exploring the city and enjoying the calm. Being in Australia made him miss home even more than he missed it when he was in Vietnam. Maybe it was all of the similarities to the States, but he longed more than ever to get out of the war and go home. He constantly thought about Shirley and the life they'd make together. He thought about traveling the USA, living in peace, cooking meals together, building a warm home and a loving family. He couldn't wait to make Shirley his bride!

Toward the end of his rest and recuperation, he decided it was time to start searching for the perfect ring. He wasn't prepared to leave Australia without one, so he spent the entire day going in and out of jewelry shops. He had been walking along the bay all morning without much luck and eventually decided it was time to leave the souvenir shops and overpriced jewelry stores behind. He headed toward King street, which he had been told by his host family was the main shopping destination in the city center. He came around a corner planning to walk down the entire length of King Street if need be, when he noticed a small blue canopy hanging over the sidewalk that read Bruce & Walsh. An hour later, he walked out of that little shop with an 18 carat white gold piece of beauty that he'd wrap around Shirley's finger. It was perfect! It had one round solitaire diamond, which Mike thought was classic and timeless. In the end, it had cost him two hundred fifty Australian dollars, which came out to slightly more than that in US dollars, but he didn't mind one bit. It was the one he had been looking for. Simple, yet elegant and beautiful. He thought it was just like Shirley's taste in things and he was sure she was going to love it.

After he paid for the ring, examining it carefully many times, he shoved the little blue box in his jacket pocket and walked around Sydney the rest of the day feeling happier than he had ever felt before. He was sure she was going to say yes, and he couldn't wait to get back to Vietnam, to see his future wife, the woman who would be the mother of his children, and give her the ring.

In the meantime, Shirley went about her days, working in the hospital, writing letters to Mike and saying constant prayers for the soldiers and for Mike's safe return from Australia. With Mike being gone, the days seemed to drag on more than usual and interestingly, they also seemed more hopeless without him. It made her wonder if the days at war were really always that hopeless, and it was just the presence of Mike, the excitement of falling in love, that made them seem more bearable. This thought gave her a deeper sense of empathy for her coworkers and friends, who were just doing their time, witnessing all of the horrors like she was, but not really having anything to look forward to at the end of a hard day. Spending all of these days alone, looking forward to Mike's return, she couldn't imagine what this year would've been like if she hadn't met him.

When Mike's plane touched back down in Vietnam, he went straight to find Shirley, without even stopping at his barracks to drop off his bags. He was so excited to see her and give her the ring, he almost couldn't stand it. When he reached her front door, he paused for a moment, took one deep breath to try to relax and then pulled the door open with haste. There she was, sitting on her bed, looking absolutely stunning!

He decided on his way to her barracks that he was not going to get down on one knee. That would immediately give it away, and he wanted to surprise her. Plus, she didn't care about things like that. He thought he'd just hand her the box, like it was a casual gift he had picked up while gone. He wanted her to be the one to open the box and see the diamond.

He knocked and then opened the door to her room before she could even answer, and to his delight, he found her alone, sitting on her bed reading a book. He burst in, barely able to contain his excitement and gave her the box without saying anything. He just stood there smiling, waiting for her to open it. "I got you something." he said in as casual a voice as he could muster, trying to downplay the whole thing, but not doing a very good job.

Shirley looked down at the little box, paused a moment to wonder what might be inside, then cracked the little velvet lid open. When she saw the ring, her expression changed from curiosity to downright thrilled. That's when Mike blurted out the question, "Will you marry me?" and all efforts to hide his pure glee were over.

Holding the box in her hand, Shirley jumped up from the bed and flung herself into his arms. "Yes! Yes, of course I will!" and with that, they shared their first kiss as fiancés. It was finally official, all their dreams about the future they would build. They were now on their way to becoming each other's family, and it could not come fast enough.

As the rainy season ended and there were more dry days than usual, the men and women stationed at Chu Lai would spend more of their time off enjoying the outdoors. They'd carefully make their way down to the little inlet of the South China Sea and wait for their turn to get in the boat or try out the skis with the doctors. It was a great way to lift their spirits and distract themselves on their days off.

WE GOTTA GET OUT OF THIS PLACE

Enjoying a day off at the beach.

On one particular such occasion, Mike and Shirley were down by the water's edge, waiting their turn to try skiing. Shirley had never done it before but she thought it looked like fun and wanted to give it a try. They waved to their friends as they skidded by on the skis, smiling and waving back to those of them hanging out on the shore. Eventually, the boat came by to pick up Mike and Shirley. Mike told her he would ride in the boat so she could try skiing first. He had been trying to give her a few pointers as they sat watching the others and waiting. She didn't know for sure if she'd be able to do it; it sounded difficult, but she wanted to at least give it a good try.

After a few brief instructions from people on the boat, she was strapped to the skis and ready to go. To Shirley, it felt like a million and one things to remember. She shook her head yes to everything, like she understood exactly what to do when the boat took off. She didn't. But she didn't want to waste any more time talking about it. In her mind, she was determined to hang on to the handlebar no matter what. She also remembered to keep the tips of her skis up toward the sky so they wouldn't get flooded.

Shirley nodded to the boat driver that she was ready. Her grip tightened on the rubber bar and as the boat jerked her forward harder than she had anticipated, she willed herself to hang on. Her mind was racing with the instructions; hold on to the grip, keep the tips of the skis upward, straighten out her legs and push the skis down, don't let go of the grip . . . she felt herself emerge from the water and she knew she had done it! She was skiing! It felt incredible to be gliding across the top of the ocean with ease, and Mike was giving her a big thumbs up from the back of the boat! She noticed that everyone on the boat was watching her, and they were all smiling and laughing, seemingly really happy that she had done so well. She felt proud that she had succeeded on her first try and she gave them all a big smile back.

After the initial shock of getting up on the skis faded, Shirley realized that something was wrong. She knew what it was before she even looked, she could feel it.

WE GOTTA GET OUT OF THIS PLACE

Continuing to hold on tightly to the grip, skating gracefully atop the water, she ventured a glance down and what she feared was confirmed. In the midst of holding on to the bar and being thrust so quickly from the water, her bathing suit top had come off! She felt heat rise to her cheeks like she never had before and looking back to the boat, Mike was clapping and laughing and giving her a huge smile and now a double thumbs up! She couldn't believe what was happening, all in a matter of seconds!

She thought for a moment about letting go of the handles and falling back into the water. But then again, the boat was going pretty fast by now and they weren't even close to the shore, and then she'd have to wade in the water by herself, topless and attached to skis, waiting for the boat to come pick her up, at which point, she'd still be topless. So, like any rational thinking person, she decided to finish out her turn on the skis and try to enjoy the thrill of it all, even if she was mortified by what was happening.

The doctor driving the boat decided to pull her by the shore a couple of times so no one hanging out on the beach would miss out on the funny story. When her turn was finally over, she sunk down into the water, letting the ocean cover her, and felt around for her missing top. Thankfully, it was around her waist and had just been pushed down by the strength of the water as she rose onto the skis, and onto the surface for all to see. Shirley quickly fastened it back into place; she was a very modest young woman, and her mind was racing with how to react to what she knew would be a storm of ceaseless teasing and joking.

She decided to be proud that she had been able to ski on her first try and take all of the joking with a good attitude. It was pretty funny, she had to admit; she just wished it hadn't been her. She knew she'd never live down that moment, as long as they were in Vietnam. The moment she accidentally went topless water skiing on the South China Sea.

As the war continued Shirley and Mike found themselves spending more time daydreaming about their futures together. Sometimes, now that they were engaged and now that they were nearing the end of their time in Vietnam, Mike would spend the night in Shirley's barracks. They couldn't stand the thought of being apart all night when the night was what little time they had to be together, and so they made the decision to break the rules.

They made sure Barb was comfortable with Mike being there overnight, and since she didn't mind, it became their new normal. Everyone on the post accepted their relationship anyway and it just didn't seem like a big deal anymore. Especially being engaged and planning a wedding for just days after they would return home, it seemed ridiculous to them to follow some silly rules that didn't apply to them anymore. They wanted to be together for the rest of their lives, no matter how short or long that would be. With the threat of incoming rockets increasing every night, they didn't want to take any chances of being killed while separated. In their minds, they were either going to leave there together or they were going to die there together.

The siren would screech in the middle of the night and everyone would jump up out of bed and take off for the bunkers. For Shirley and Mike, their bunker was just at the bottom of the barracks where they slept, and they'd run down the steps into the sunken room. The entire thing was made of sandbags and lined with two long benches facing each other. Everyone would pile in toward the back, away from the opening, and in their pajamas they'd pass the time with conversation. At times, they'd hear the explosions going off outside and would feel apprehensive, taking shallow breaths as if waiting to be hit by a rocket at any moment.

Eventually the sounds would stop and everyone would take a full breath, beginning to relax. The time they stayed down in the sandbag haven varied, sometimes only 30 minutes, and sometimes a couple of hours. They'd wait for the all clear, indicated by a different siren and then they would migrate back to their rooms, and try to get some sleep before they had to start saving lives again.

Just a couple of days after the future Hensleys' exciting engagement took place, the war abruptly and viciously snapped them back to reality, as if to remind them of where they were. It struck them in a way it hadn't yet, in a way they had not expected. Though seasoned by ten months of seeing suffering and death on a daily basis, nothing could have prepared them for what came next.

On March 28, 1971 in the Quang Tin Province of South Vietnam, a group of about 50 Viet Cong sappers forged a surprise attack on the American Fire Support Base (FSB) Mary Ann. Sappers were Vietnamese special task forces who operated stealthily to carry out deadly attacks on enemy troops. They were supplied with grenades, satchel charges, and an AK-47 or RPG-7. They traveled light, which made them highly mobile and able to move in on their targets quickly, using the element of surprise to their advantage.

In the early morning hours of that day, while most soldiers were sleeping, the Viet Cong sappers carefully clipped their way through concertina wires, quietly waded through the protective trenches and began a close range ground attack against the Americal 1-46th infantry division. There had been such a decrease in battle activity in the area surrounding Mary Ann that it came as a total shock to the Americans. They had become lax over the past few weeks of relative peace they had been enjoying, preparing to turn the FSB over to the ARVN in about a month's time. The sappers saw it as the perfect opportunity to do grave damage (Bell, 2006).

WE GOTTA GET OUT OF THIS PLACE

Shortly after the attack began, the news reached Chu Lai by radio that FSB Mary Ann needed medevac choppers; they were currently being attacked and they badly needed outside support. They were suffering heavy casualties and were still fighting to regain control of their base. Mike was working his night shift in the OR at the hospital when the call came in. When he heard that the guys from the Americal 1-46th infantry division were the ones being attacked, he felt ice begin to crawl up his back, the little hairs on his neck stood at attention, and he went numb.

Even though he was just finishing his 12-hour shift, he immediately approached his CO and asked permission to ride in a dust off headed for Mary Ann. The CO looked at him like he was being foolish and told him that the hospital would need all hands on deck, to stay put and wait for soldiers to arrive.

Usually, Mike would stand down and obey orders, but that night, his voice shook in his throat, his face flushed red, and he asked again. More urgently the second time. He tried desperately to help his CO understand that those guys at Mary Ann, the Americal 1-46th ID, that was his unit! Those were his guys! He had to go, he had to! The CO paused, registering the look of confusion and panic, the hurt and the urgency in Mike's voice, and he understood. He had to go, those were his guys.

He told Mike he could go, but not to think he'd be getting a break when he got back. They'd still need all hands operating and that included him. He'd come back from doing dust off and he'd go straight into surgery. As long as he understood those terms, he could go.

Mike didn't say another word. He glanced quickly at Shirley who was standing nearby, watching the whole conversation, and graciously, she shook her head to signal that she understood; he needed to go. Mike returned the nod to let her know he'd be alright, he'd be back. And with that, he took off running toward the helipad to jump in the first medevac he could find that had room. He knew many of the guys at Mary Ann would need the attention of a medic before they arrived back at the hospital, and the few medics out there would probably be overwhelmed with this large of an attack. The guys in the chopper Mike jumped into were happy to have a medic join them, as they were just two guys, a pilot and copilot, going up to Mary Ann to bring back the injured.

As the chopper came in to land at Mary Ann just after daybreak, Mike could begin to see some of the horrors that took place. Smoke rose from the earth, black and grey swirls clouding the air. Fire still burned in some of the broken structures. The smell of charred earth and flesh filled his nostrils and for the first time since jumping on the medevac, he wondered if the raid was truly over.

The fighting had pretty much ceased by the time the Chu Lai Hueys made it to Mary Ann. The place looked like hell. Mike jumped from the chopper side door, as it touched down, and ran from under the blades as they cut the stale air. For a moment, he stood there paralyzed in complete and utter shock. The scene was chilling. He had never witnessed anything like it, and he would never see anything like it ever again. He glanced around in all directions, trying to gather his thoughts, trying to figure out what to do. This was not what he expected to find when he jumped in that dust off. As he was taking it all in, he noticed that he wasn't the only one frozen in place. Those whom he had traveled with, seemed to be experiencing the same sort of stupor and confusion. Mike was a medic, and he had come expecting to find injured soldiers that he could begin treating. Instead, the bodies laid still.

From the helipad, a somewhat steep hill descended down to where the brunt of the attack had taken place. Mike could see a few commanding officers standing around talking, studying the massacre and trying to come up with a plan. He also saw some soldiers walking around in a daze with blood dripping from their heads, loose bandages poorly doing their job. The corpsman had all been killed in the attack, so there were no properly trained men around to help these guys. Medics who had come before Mike had focused on the most needy, saving lives and evacuating the men to either the 27th surgical hospital, which was closer to the action but a smaller operation, or the 91st evacuation hospital back in Chu Lai.

After his brief moment of intake, all of his senses registering the severity of what actually took place just hours ago, his military training took over and he moved into action. He walked over to the group of officers and asked them what he could do to help. They were at a loss for words, bewildered by the horrific scene in which they found themselves, and told Mike to help anyone he saw that was injured. Mike looked around but only saw a few guys who had already been treated and were just walking around in shock. He decided to head down the hill, into the main attack site.

As he made his way down, he noticed one of the enemy sappers lying still on his back. Across his chest, strapped to his body, were unexploded bombs. Mike looked at his face to make sure he was dead, the hairs raised on the back of his neck and he realized for the first time that going there to help could cost him his life. What if one of the enemies wasn't really dead and they were waiting to detonate their chest satchel bombs to kill one more American before they died? What if when he got close enough to them, they'd sense it and blow him to pieces? Mike looked around at the bodies and he feared becoming like them.

The soldiers' bodies, laid dismembered and scattered across the dirt. Mike knew they would need to be brought home to their loved ones. They would need to be boxed in a coffin, flown home and buried beneath a white cross. The remains of these men would need to be saved, so they could be honored as the fallen heros they were. He pushed any fears that threatened to cripple, deep down and came up with his own plan of action.

There were body bags on board the chopper, though maybe not enough for the casualties he was facing. He decided the best way to help would be to collect the body parts, and place them in the bags to be brought back to the morgue. His initial plan was to try to figure out which pieces belonged together and put them in a pile with each other at the edge of the helipad. He'd carry the dead limbs up the hill, place them as gently and with as much care and respect as possible and then head back down until they were all saved from that God forsaken land. He would not leave anyone behind.

He went to work, trying incredibly hard to identify limbs that might belong with torsos, and heads strewn about the land. Sometimes it was impossible to tell which members were one body and which were another. It was not only physically taxing, hiking up and down the hill, carrying extremely heavy bodies, but the mental and emotional strain of trying to respect these young men, as he retrieved pieces of them and put them in a pile, was almost unbearable.

After a short time, he realized that he had more body parts than bodies. Somehow he was able to think clearly enough to realize that some of the arms, legs, hands, and feet he was finding belonged to the survivors. Guys who had already been evacuated to hospitals and would be missing these pieces for the rest of their lives.

He continued to collect the men, but between hiking up and down the hill, carrying the bodies, trying to match blown apart pieces, and watching out for sappers, it became too much. The extra body parts made it too difficult to put whole men back together. His plan was not working; he couldn't figure out who was who. He wouldn't leave anyone behind though, so he just started gathering all the parts he could find and bringing them to the helipad. From that point on, they'd all go in one pile. He was sorry for it, but he couldn't put them back together, and he knew he needed to get over it and move on. His new mantra became, "Just bring them all home." It was a good plan, and it worked.

For Mike, this felt like one of the most important things he had done yet in the war. Sweat was dripping from his face, mud was on his boots and pants, and he had blood all over his hands and fatigues. When he had left in such haste from the hospital, he hadn't even grabbed a bag of supplies. He figured there'd be some on the chopper, and there were some, but not even a pair of gloves. Mike had carried each man up that hill with his bare hands.

After one of his very heavy loads up the hill, he ran back down to the bottom and stopped to catch his breath. The heaviness of those body parts was surprising to him. He had never felt anything so weighty in his entire life and it seemed shocking that these remnants of men could weigh so much. He walked around to catch his breath, standing still was too uncomfortable, and as he crossed over a dirt walkway, he heard someone cry out in a loud and powerful voice, "Fire in the hole!"

Mike reacted so quickly, desperately wanting to avoid becoming the pieces he had just cleaned up. To his right side, there was a large crater, which had most likely been carved out by an explosion during the battle. Without hesitation he dove headfirst over the dirt wall and into the hole. As he fell in the pit, his body slammed against another man who was taking cover in the same crater. Mike, filthy and bloodied from the work he had been doing all morning, immediately noticed the firmly pressed crease down the shoulder line of the man's sleeve. As Mike's eyes scanned up the uniform, clean and freshly starched, he saw numerous colorful badges stitched perfectly to the chest, four stars lined each shoulder and beneath them, the name tag read, Abrams.

Army General Creighton W. Abrams, Jr. was sharing Mike's hole. Mike, an enlisted boy from Ft. Lauderdale, FL, jumped into a crater with the Commander of the Vietnam War. Mike looked into his eyes with a different kind of bewilderment. General Abrams asked Mike if he was okay, something like, "What's going on, son? Is everything ok?"

Mike responded that he didn't know what was happening, just heard someone yell out "Fire in the hole" and that a sapper may still be alive. He then remembered to add, "Sir" to make sure he gave proper respect.

Abrams and Mike stood up, nothing had come of the supposed sapper attack. It was a false alarm. Both a bit shaken, they brushed off their uniforms and climbed out of the hole. General Abrams went one way and Mike went back from where he had come to continue cleaning up his fallen comrades. His unit.

After a couple of hours, Mike finally finished gathering all of the men. He climbed to the top of the hill for the last time, standing to look out over the site. He had seen it all. Detached heads, eyes still staring at him, fogging over with the glaze of death. He had seen flesh and bones independent of their limbs, just lying in the dirt. Torsos, alone. Arms, legs, organs . . . he had picked it all up and carried them to the helipad with his bare hands.

His body and fatigues were blackened with matted blood. He wiped the sweat from his forehead, leaving a streak of dark red on his own skin and scanned the base one last time. Mindlessly lifting his end of the body bags into the chopper, he didn't say a word. Just helped the pilots get the guys loaded up. Mike eventually climbed aboard the aircraft, and surrounded by the black bags, he rode in silence as they made their way back to Chu Lai.

The whole ride back to the post, he thought he'd never forget that day. He'd never forget sitting in the back of that chopper, sharing the space with all those dead men. He'd never forget the fear he felt when he thought a sapper was about to attack him, and he'd never forget the weight. The unbelievably heavy, dead weight of those men that he carried home. He'd never forget that. And as the chopper cut toward Chu Lai, he knew this day would haunt him the rest of his life.

The choppers had been under fire, making hot landings to pick up the wounded and dead. As Mike and the guys left, more shots were fired into FSB Mary Ann and another American was shot and wounded (Bell, 2006).

The huey landed at Chu Lai some 45 minutes later and Mike staggered into the hospital to find Shirley. He had never in his young life experienced something so horrific, so unexplainable, so shattering. He could find no words to describe what he was feeling, he just knew he needed to see the woman he loved. He walked into the ICU, saw her working feverishly with the other nurses and doctors, and headed straight for her.

Shirley had been hearing choppers come in one after the other, bringing the largest number of guys they had yet seen at any given time. She thought that they must've seen at least 40 men come in so far, all needing life saving surgeries, treatments and medicines. She was working as fast and as hard as she could to help every soldier in her reach. It was completely chaotic at times as new waves of medevacs would land and they'd have more critically injured men coming in before they were even able to take care of the last bunch.

Her mind kept drifting to Mike. She knew he was out there, seeing all of this where it happened. Maybe helping some of these very men she was helping now. She worried about him so much, but wouldn't allow herself to focus on it. Instead, she focused on her work, on the men in front of her. But at the same time, the man she loved might be in danger, and she felt great fear for him. She hadn't even heard if the battle was over. Was Mike's chopper being fired upon? Were enemies still attacking? Was he having to use his gun? She prayed and prayed for his safety and worked harder than she had all war.

She heard more medevacs landing outside and every time, she'd watch the door for a moment to see if he was back. She glanced at the doors and waited for a second. When he didn't come in, she went back to work, keeping her mind busy with her tasks. A minute later, another nurse said her name in a way that grabbed her immediate attention, and when Shirley looked up, the nurse gestured for her to look behind her. She turned around just in time to see Mike approaching, and her heart just filled with all kinds of delight and sadness at the sight of him. She was beyond thankful to see him alive and, though covered in blood, she could tell that he was uninjured physically by the way he was walking and looking around for her. Their eyes connected from across the room, and she could see by the look that came over his face that he had just been to hell and back. She directed him to step into a side room with her, and there, he lost himself.

He grabbed onto her tight, pulling her into an embrace and sinking his head into her shoulder. He sobbed like he never had before in his entire life. He hurt so bad, his lungs, his chest, his heart, his mind. It didn't seem real and he could not comprehend how anyone sitting in an office halfway around the world could choose this end for someone they had never met.

He couldn't speak, but just wept and kept shaking his head. He couldn't understand the purpose, the waste of good lives, the senselessness. Those guys out there lived with a fear so intense it could kill all on its own. He had just felt it. This wasn't right and he didn't know what to do.

Shirley held him without asking questions or talking. She was just there with him. A wisdom she possessed beyond her years, took over and comforted him with her understanding and her presence. She didn't care that he was all bloody and dirty and sweaty. She didn't care that he was touching her hair and her skin with hands covered in blood that wasn't even his own. She didn't care about anything except being present for the man she loved. He needed her to be strong, so he could be weak.

After a few minutes of allowing the emotions to drain out, he composed himself and looked her in the eyes. They shared a moment of heartache together, both glassy-eyed and sorrowful in spirit. They said a few encouraging words to one another and decided it'd be best for them to both get back to work. Shirley watched him walk away, and she couldn't help but notice how he looked different. He had seen the worst of humanity, he had held it in his hands and he was older now. He had aged years from the last time she had seen him, just hours ago. It broke her heart.

Mike walked to the OR and straight into the surgical prep room. He was more filthy than he had been in a very long time, possibly ever, and he needed to get ready for surgery in sterile environments. He took the soap, and with the hot water pouring out of the pipes, began to scrub his arms and hands, all the way past the elbows. As he did, the blood of the men he had brought back, washed down the drain. He watched it, scrubbing it free from his skin, running down the walls of the sink, mixing with the water and bubbles, and out of sight.

He scrubbed harder and harder and faster until there was just a tiny bit of his comrades' blood left. Then he slowed down, realizing that this was the last trace of life from those men. Their lifeblood, now dead and caked onto him, wanted to be remembered. He took a moment and washed the last bit away, slowly, respectfully, he thought.

WE GOTTA GET OUT OF THIS PLACE

He made sure to follow it with his eyes all the way down, vowing never to forget their sacrifice. He watched it disappear with the suds through the drain, and he felt an enormous sense of loss. The loss of their lives, finalized. The loss of their weight, gone from him. He was no longer carrying their lives on his own flesh; they were gone.

After all of the blood and dirt was carefully scrubbed away, he changed into fresh scrubs and a full surgical gown. He took a deep breath, walked into the operating room and began assisting with surgeries.

Chapter Eight

SHORT TIMERS

Short calendars were hand-drawn countdowns to home. Soldiers called them short calendars because it showed them how short of a time they had left to serve in this horrible war. A 365-day countdown to their escape from hell. Every day they survived, they got to color in another little box, and when all the tiny boxes were colored in, the calendar would boldly read "HOME." It was a much needed visual reminder to have hope for their futures. A soldier wasn't really even considered short until he or she had less than 100 days to go. After that, they were considered a two-digit midget, which was getting really short. Then a one-digit midget, which was as short as a person could be. One-digit midgets were already gone mentally, dreaming of the stars and stripes, old friends and family, and good ol' US soil under foot.

Mike and Shirley's hand drawn "Short" calendar.

As Mike and Shirley became increasingly shorter, plans for their upcoming nuptials began to form. They decided on the date of July 3, 1971 for their wedding because Shirley's family would already be gathering together for the fourth of July. This date was just ten days after they would arrive home from war. Since Shirley had arrived in the country a whole month before Mike's arrival, she decided to extend her tour in Vietnam by one month so they could go home together. For being in Vietnam longer than 12 months, she was granted a second R&R. This time, she decided to go to Hong Kong, China with some of the other nurses. She would be spending a week in China just before her return to the United States. Since the wedding was less than two weeks after their homecoming, she wanted to buy their wedding bands, her wedding dress, and bridesmaid dresses while she had time to do some shopping in Hong Kong.

Over the weeks leading up to her China trip, Shirley began making phone calls home any time the USO was on post and the phones were open. Over her year in Vietnam, she had come to forgive her dad for his past behavior and she realized how much she missed her mom and siblings. She wanted to come back to the states and give her relationship with her family a fresh start. She wanted them to be involved in her wedding and to meet Mike. She had big hopes that they could all start over.

Shirley planned the whole wedding from Vietnam through telephone calls to her sisters and Mike's family. She had decided on her three bridesmaids and gathered their dress sizes because she wanted to pick out their dresses in Hong Kong. They had chosen to make a potluck dinner and had decided upon who would bring what dishes. They chose the pastor and the venue and came up with an invitation list. Every detail was figured out over the phone, half a world away from where this dreamy day would take place. It wasn't easy being so far away from her sisters and family in all the excitement of planning, but she was filled with excitement nonetheless.

Right from the start of her trip to Hong Kong, she was keeping her eyes out for wedding rings, wedding dresses,

SHORT TIMERS

and bridesmaid dresses. As the girls were walking by some shops one day, Shirley noticed in the window a beautiful, delicate looking dress with ruffles and lace. What drew her attention to it in the first place were the colors. This dress was a combination of lovely bold colors; blues, greens, purples, pinks, yellows, all in a tie-dyed pattern! All throughout the sixties Shirley had loved the tie-dye style, and to find it done so nicely on this full length gown was absolutely perfect.

The girls ran in the shop to see if there were more than one of these fabulous dresses. They were delighted to find out that it was a popular style, and there were lots of them in stock. They also had wedding dresses, and Shirley fell in love with a delicate, long sleeved, lacy gown. It didn't take long until they had found all three sizes Shirley was looking for. She bought her wedding gown and the tie-dyed beauties and left the store with a more complete picture of what her wedding was going to look like. Tie-dye bridesmaid dresses from China... she would've never dreamed of such a thing as a child when picturing her wedding day, and yet, it was better than any dream she could've come up with on her own. The dresses, the rings, the potluck wedding... it was all better than she could've ever wished.

As the week went on, Shirley and her nurse friends enjoyed lots of delicious Chinese cuisine and more shopping. Everything felt drastically different in a peacetime environment and Shirley couldn't wait to get home in a month and start building a life of peace together with Mike. Her mind was all over the place, dreaming of the future they would build with one another.

As the girls walked into a particular shop, Shirley noticed the jewelry section had plain silver rings. She found out they were actually white gold wedding bands and they were quite affordable. There was a matching set of a man's and a woman's wedding ring. The man's ring was wider, thicker, and heavier looking, and the woman's ring was petite and narrow . . . she fell in love with them. These were the matching bands that the two lovers would give to each other on their wedding day. The store would even engrave them for free. It was perfect!

Shirley purchased the rings for 30 dollars and had each one engraved. Hers read peace and his read together. Peace together had become their relationship mantra. It was their mission as a couple; to create it, to build it. It was their hope for their marriage and their future, the treasure they'd hunt for and the one they'd find, peace together . . . it meant more to them than just mere words or a phrase. It was a shared dream, a sustaining hope for their love and what they could accomplish with it.

Shirley wrapped the rings in tissue paper and stuck them in her purse. She was thrilled to have found them for such a great price and couldn't wait to show Mike. The rest

SHORT TIMERS

of the week she relaxed with the girls, enjoying her time away from work.

When Shirley arrived back at the post, they only had three weeks of the war left. Their short calendar was so close to being fully filled. They began to believe it was actually going to happen, they were actually going to make it home together, they were going to leave Vietnam, get back to the world and start the rest of their lives. All the things they had been dreaming about together were seeming more and more possible. They were so close to home they could almost taste it! And yet, the bomb threats were increasing. Their time in the bunker seemed to be getting longer and longer and they feared, as many short soldiers did, that they'd be killed just before their time was up.

There was a paranoia with soldiers who had reached their last weeks and days in the war, that home would never come. That it was just a cruel trick. A mirage. That it was too good to be true, because after a year at war, nothing good was ever true. The only truth they knew was that death was imminent, and it would not let them leave. Just as it hadn't let their comrades leave. Some soldiers would get so skittish in their last days, certain that the grim reaper would be hiding just around the bend, that they became unreasonably fearful of doing certain tasks they had been doing for an entire year. They no longer wanted to leave the post for the orphanage, or let their hooch maids clean their barracks. They became convinced that their last guard duty shift would get them killed or that they'd be bombed while hiding out in their bunkers. It was a terrible feeling and one that drove many short timers a little crazy.

Mike and Shirley didn't want to let fear run their lives when they became short. They decided to celebrate their short timer status by taking one of their sleep days to go on a one-day R&R in the country. Infantry soldiers were awarded a three-day, in-country R&R and they'd usually be sent to Da Nang, where the Army had built barracks near the beach.

Shirley and Mike had both heard of the wide open beaches, the cold beer, and the good food that came with that small break from war. Feeling the need to get away from the hospital, they hurried out to the helipad to bum a chopper ride. The pilots were more than willing to have them on board, and without hesitation, they jumped in the slick, took a seat behind the door gunner on a mesh bench and headed for Da Nang. There was plenty of room as they flew the 90 miles northward since they were the only ones on the chopper besides the gunner and two pilots. They were looking forward to spending the whole day off together relaxing at a beautiful beach.

SHORT TIMERS

Shirley standing in front of a Medevac chopper named Tired Angel.

Leaving the compound, they had to fly over enemy-occupied territory to get north to Da Nang. The Hueys were incredibly loud and there was no hiding the fact that they were up there. Soldiers on the ground would be able to hear them coming.

The chopper flew low and fast, to be less visible, staying just above the treetops. This made it much more difficult for enemies to strike them down with firepower, as they wouldn't get a visual on the bird until it was just over their heads. Then they'd have to rush to aim and get their shots off, and usually, that meant they'd miss. If the choppers flew well above the treetops, they'd have no cover, and the enemy would have ample time to aim and shoot them down.

While Mike and Shirley didn't like being so low to the ground, they were enjoying the ride. It was rare that they ever got to experience the country from that perspective, and Shirley dug her camera out to snap some aerial photos.

As they went about their route, Mike heard a terrifying sound coming from below. He was pretty sure what he was hearing, and the pilot confirmed it for them. The pilot looked back at Shirley and Mike, sitting close to one another and told them the chopper was being fired upon. The sound of bullets whizzing by as enemies were opening fire on them from the ground was ringing in their ears. The door gunner returned fire in the direction of the bullets and the pilot yelled back for them to hang on. Enemy bullets sprayed over the tail of the bird as the pilot made a quick maneuver to avoid being hit. The huey rolled to the right side, dropped for a moment and then rose with a ferocity that made Mike's heart sink into his stomach.

Mike and Shirley were not used to this type of activity at all. Even though she refused to let fear completely cripple her mind, Shirley felt an intense spell of emotions as her chest turned to stone. Within seconds, there was that old paranoia about being so short on remaining days, nagging at her heart and mind, making her regret that they had ever left the safety of the post. The shots continued to fly up to the chopper, and Shirley interlocked her fingers with Mike's, squeezing tight, holding his eyes with hers while the blades chopped the air and the bullets hit the trees. They sat in silence until the firing could no longer be heard, holding their breaths, saying a few prayers. The bullets never made a single hit.

The pilot gracefully landed the huey in Da Nang, unharmed. Mike and Shirley were a little emotionally shaken, but quickly got over it, as they looked out at the neverending beach. They knew all they had was the moment they were living, no more wasting time thinking about that ride up there. They said, "It don't mean nothing" and smiled at the new and beautiful scenery.

Soldiers in Vietnam often said that phrase about things that were too heavy for them to deal with emotionally. Usually, the more it meant, the more they'd say it didn't mean anything. They used it to cope with hard situations, like when they had a soldier whose life was lost on the operating table, like when they ran to the bunker from incoming mortars, like getting shot at in the chopper. . . . They'd parrot the old phrase, wrapping it around their hearts like a security blanket, "It don't mean nothing." And they were right. It meant everything.

The powdery white sand on the beach in Da Nang seemed to stretch on for miles, as far as the eye could see in either direction. They kicked off their boots, felt the sand between their toes and walked along the beautiful South China Sea holding hands. They had left Chu Lai in such haste, after making the spontaneous decision to go to Da Nang, and consequently they were at the beach without their swimsuits.

The more they walked along the water, the more they wanted to get in. It was hot outside and the sea looked so refreshing, sparkly blue and inviting. At once, Shirley tossed her boots into the sand and started pulling Mike toward the water, fully clothed. He threw his boots next to hers and together they plunged into the waves fully dressed in their fatigues! Living in the moment was a way of life in Vietnam. They didn't think, they didn't hesitate, they just did what felt right. Who knew if they'd ever have another moment to be alive together, so they'd better make the most of it while there was a chance.

After swimming together for a while, laughing, splashing each other and flirting, they drug themselves out of the water, drenched and heavy with the ocean, and relaxed in the sun, letting the breeze wash over them. It was almost as if they were on a real date, back home, not living in the middle of a war. It was just so nice to get away from the post and spend an entire day together, even if they had risked their lives to get there.

Top: On the beach in Da Nang after swimming in the ocean. Bottom: Enjoying lunch before heading back to Chu Lai.

They ended up following their noses to find the small, beachside restaurant for lunch they had been hearing about from other soldiers. Their time in Da Nang was so peaceful, it almost seemed like the country itself was not at war. It was really depressing, to see what it could be like without all of the bloodshed and fighting. It could be beautiful. It could be paradise.

As the time came for them to catch their ride back to Chu Lai, they felt their muscles stiffen back up, wondering if they would be shot at on their way home also. Wondering if they had any luck left. The old nagging questions returned, how could they have risked it? They were so close to going home, why did they leave the post just for one day?

They made it safely back to Chu Lai without a shot.

As they entered their last week at war, their hearts struggled to hang on to hope that they'd make it home alive. And for good reason! It seemed as though every single night the siren would scream, warning them of incoming rockets. They'd wake in a hurry, rush down the barracks steps and into the bunker. They knew the enemy was capable of launching bombs that far into their post from the coast and even though hospitals were supposed to be left alone in battles, there was never a guarantee that the enemy would follow the rules of war. They knew that just one year before their arrival, bombs had rained down on the hospital in Chu Lai and an Army nurse was killed.

Each time that siren would wake them from their slumber, they'd feel more and more anxious that this was the end. That their happily ever after would remain unfinished. They'd grab each other's hand, hold on tightly, and run beneath the sandbags. Down in the dark of that room, Shirley would silently pray for their protection, for them to be saved from this evil. If evil prevailed, they comforted themselves with the fact that at least they'd go together. If at any second, all hell broke loose, and bombs rained down on them, the sandbags becoming their tomb, at least they'd get to hold each other in their last moments, their hearts covering one another in love. Having experienced true love, however short of a period it had been . . . it was enough to die at peace, together.

SHORT TIMERS

Thankfully, even though the threat of incoming bombs increased in frequency over their last days, nothing ever happened. They began packing the few belongings they had, in preparation for their upcoming departure from war. They had been so busy saying their goodbyes to friends that they hadn't even been filling in their short calendar. Shirley peeled it off the wall of her barracks, unfinished, and carefully stowed it away. She thought it would be something neat she and Mike could show their kids and grandkids one day.

On their last weekend, despite their fears, they hopped aboard the truck to the orphanage. They had to see Ching Chong one last time. As they rode through the streets of the village, they smiled wide at one another, letting the sun soak their skin. They remembered the first time they had ridden in the back of that truck, nearly nine months earlier. Getting on that truck was the best decision either of them had ever made. That truck introduced them to each other. That dirty, wooden railed, deuce and a half . . . they wanted to remember it and so they rode in silence the rest of the way, watching the town and thinking about the good fortune they had found on that very journey they were making for the last time.

At the school, they found Ching Chong, played with him as long as they could, and left feeling heartbroken that they'd never see him again. Shirley prayed for him, for his future, for his life. She hoped it would be long and happy and healthy. She knew she'd always remember him; for as long as she lived, she'd remember him and she'd love him. It was hard leaving him, not being able to explain to him that they wouldn't see each other again. She squeezed him tight and kissed him on the top of his head, glassy eyed and conflicted.

As she climbed back in the truck, Mike scooped him up and gave him the biggest, longest bear hug. Ching Chong loved them both, and rewarded their affection with a huge smile and tight embrace. Mike set him down, hoping in his heart that Ching Chong would see a peaceful and bright future. He had never wanted good things for someone so badly before, and he wished very deeply, that by some kind of miracle, that sweet baby boy's life would turn out happily, full of love and belonging.

With those final thoughts, Mike got in the truck and as they pulled away for the last time, chased down by all the little ones. They kept their eyes on Ching Chong, standing there smiling at them and waving. They watched him until they couldn't see him anymore, the truck carrying them away, out of his life, back to the post for their last days in Vietnam....

Shirley and Mike worked their final shift at the hospital. By this time, they were both working the day shift, 7 am to 7 pm. As they went about their duties, they were very aware of the fact that this would be their last time doing these tasks at the Chu Lai 91st evacuation hospital. The last time they'd work to save lives in the Vietnam War. It was bittersweet. A strange tinge of sadness about leaving Vietnam was mixed in with all of the positive feelings. It was confusing and it didn't seem to make sense, but it was there, underneath it all, lying deep in the pit of their souls. Did they really deserve to leave? Had they done enough? Would their friends, who were staying behind, be alright without them? Should they feel guilty about going home when they met so many who hadn't been so lucky? Would anyone know what they had gone through and would they be able to have meaningful relationships with people who had never been to war?

They contemplated all of these deep questions together, working through the confusion of feeling negative emotions about leaving, when that was what they had been waiting for since they had arrived. It was hard to understand; they felt that not only was the war losing them, but they were losing the war. It wouldn't be theirs anymore, at least not in the ways it had been over the last year. From now on, they would be powerless to help their fellow soldiers in need. Eventually they came to the conclusion that leaving war is a loss too, not one that can be explained or understood, but a loss that must be mourned as well as celebrated.

They collected the glass IV bottles for disposal on their last shift and walked over to the coast. They made their way down to the place where everyone threw the bottles onto the rocks, and they took turns pitching the glass into the earth one last time. The shattered shards provided the post with a little bit of extra protection against invading enemies trying to climb the rocks up from the ocean. This was something Mike and Shirley enjoyed doing together over the past year. Looking out at the South China Sea and breaking the glass bottles against the cliffs. They had had many great conversations over the months, doing that very thing in that very spot. As they came to the last bottle, they paused to smile at one another, and Shirley told Mike to throw it. He gripped the glass firmly, looked out at the sea, listening to the waves crash and said, "Goodbye, Vietnam! We're never coming back!"

And with that, he launched the last bottle over the cliff.

Throwing glass bottles over the cliff.

SHORT TIMERS

The sun rose, bringing to light their final day in Vietnam. The last day, the day they'd be boarding a plane bound for home, and they'd never have to look back. Pat and Barb had left the month before, and Shirley was looking forward to seeing them again in the States. Before heading to the air strip, they made their rounds to say their final goodbyes to the friends they had made and their coworkers. Everyone congratulated them on getting to go back home and sent them off with well wishes.

Mike carried their olive drab green hard cases to the long line waiting to board the plane. Officers were in the front of the line, as always, and enlisted men were in the back. However, now that Mike was Shirley's fiancé, he was standing at the front of line with her. As they watched all the new soldiers, green with innocence, file off the aircraft to begin their yearlong deployment, Mike couldn't help remembering when he was one of them. It seemed a lifetime ago. He had been so young, so fresh, and inexperienced. Just a kid out of high school. Now, he had been living in a foreign country at war for a year, had saved lives, had lost lives, had seen the aftermath of terrible battles and had met the woman he was going to marry. He was going home a man, and he felt it.

Looking at the fresh faces, it was hard to believe he had only been gone a year. He knew that somehow, he had grown and matured more than any other year of his life thus far. He imagined it was all the extremes he was dealing with. Life and death, elation and devastation, love and hate, peace and war . . . he had experienced all of these opposites in the most severe ways over his year in Vietnam, and he guessed it had produced an expedited growth in him. He began wondering if he'd be able to relate to any people his own age back home who had not come to the war. Would they be too innocent, too ignorant? All he knew at that moment was that he was going home with Shirley and in ten days time, she would be his bride. He knew that at least they'd understand each other, even if no one else did, they'd know what they've been through and they would always have that bond.

Shirley could also remember being fresh to the war. She recalled the intense nerves she felt for being a few days behind Barb and hoping to meet up with her as soon as possible. She thought about how her senses were shocked by all of the new sounds of war and the foreign smells, how it caused her to feel great fear and second guess her decision to request orders she knew would get her sent to Vietnam. But it had all worked out. It had all been for a purpose, she knew, and though the war was tremendously scarring, she was glad she came. She had helped thousands of soldiers in need, had prayed over many souls, made new friends and even met her future husband. It was worth it.

As their turn finally came to get on the plane, they made their way up the staircase to the door. Each soldier was stopped and carefully checked off on an attendance sheet before boarding. When it came time for them to state their names, the men gave Mike a disapproving look. They did not like that an enlisted man was getting on the plane ahead of some other officers, but since he was with Shirley, there was nothing they could do.

They hesitated a moment and then said that the officer and her gentleman could board the plane. The rest of the way home, at each checkpoint, they were referred to as the officer and her husband! Even though they weren't quite married yet, they were close enough to feel comfortable with the term, and they wanted to be sure they'd get to stay together. Mike and Shirley thought this was wildly entertaining, to see the looks they got, the initial pause, the eyebrow raises from military personnel and the smirking headshakes.

They didn't say a word, just followed directions and stayed together. Shirley made a mental note to herself to never let Mike live down the fact that he was referred to as her gentleman and she was his superior. In this fashion, they made their way all the way home, back to the land they loved and missed.

They landed at Sea-Tac (Seattle-Tacoma) airport and were taken directly to Fort Lewis for their homecoming, processing, and if applicable, decommissioning. They were delighted to find that Vietnam veterans were being welcomed home with a steak dinner. They couldn't believe it. They had been eating MREs, also known as shit on a brick, and cafeteria food for a whole year. And there, right in front of them, was a juicy steak dinner, for free! It was the best steak either of them had ever tasted.

After their bellies were sufficiently full, they split up so Mike could get new dress greens and Shirley could process out of the military. She had served in the Army for three years, eight months, and fourteen days. She was ready to move on from the military and make a career as a civilian nurse. Mike and Shirley met back up and Barb, who had arrived home from the war just days before they did, came to pick them up from the base. They would be flying to Cincinnati the next day, and Barb let them stay at her place just outside Seattle for the night.

Mike had made the decision to serve one more year with the Army, and had received orders to go to Germany. As the wedding was quickly approaching, Mike and Shirley discussed the pros and cons of moving to Europe for a year. After having been away from the States for so long, and having just returned, neither of them were very excited about turning around and leaving again to live in a foreign country. Plus, even though they would be officially married by that time, there was no guarantee that the military would provide private housing for the newlywed couple, or even housing for Shirley at all. Pretty quickly, they decided that if Mike could get a change of orders, that'd be best. He remembered someone saying that soldiers could get their orders changed at the Pentagon in Washington, D.C., and he thought it was worth a shot.

When they landed in Ohio, Mike immediately booked a flight to Maryland for the next day. He didn't have much time before the wedding to get those orders changed, so he figured he'd better go sooner than later. Shirley would stay in Ohio with her family and continue to prepare for the wedding, and Mike would go alone to the Pentagon.

He walked off the plane and found his way to the Pentagon. Not sure exactly where to go or who to speak to, he walked in wearing his full dress greens and told a receptionist that someone told him he could get his orders changed there. She looked him up and down and said he could try a certain office, handed him a map of the building, and pointed him off. He walked through corridor after corridor, trying his best to follow the map. He got lost a couple of times, went down more halls and doors, and felt like he was inside a maze.

Eventually, he saw a half door, with a sign sticking out above that read, "Change of orders." He found it. His first obstacle was down, and if he could just get his orders changed, the trip would be a huge success. The person behind the half door studied him for a second and then let him inside. He was met by an older gentleman, who asked him what he wanted.

Mike replied, and the man asked him where he was coming from and where his new orders were sending him. Mike looked down at the orders he was holding in his hand and told the man he was coming from Vietnam, ordered to go to Germany. He told him he was getting married in a couple of days and would really like to stay in the country. When Mike was finished with his brief request, the man looked him straight in the eyes and said, "Where do you want to go, soldier?"

Taken aback, not having expected that kind of response, he gasped and asked if the man was serious. The man was absolutely serious, and asked Mike again where he would like to go. He thought for a moment and in his shock and amazement at how well it was all going, he said he guessed it'd be nice to be near home. He didn't even have time to call Shirley. The man helped Mike find a location as close to his home as possible, as he had requested. He walked out of the Pentagon with freshly printed orders in his hand. In a months' time, he'd be reporting to Atlanta, Georgia. Mike knew he was being appreciated for having served in Vietnam, and it felt so unbelievably good.

When he had put on his dress greens to travel for the meeting, he had received disapproving looks from citizens in the airports, stares filled with hate, and people even being so bold as to spit on the ground in front of him. At least they didn't spit on him, like he knew some other fellow soldiers had experienced. It made him so mad though, because he hadn't even been fighting in the war, just helping wounded people, American and enemy alike! But people were looking at him like he was a murderer, like he should be completely ashamed of himself for being involved in the military at all, even to help.

He didn't really care about their opinions too much, because they weren't there and they didn't know what they were talking about, but on some level, it still bothered him. It didn't feel good to come home to people hating him and wishing ill on him. It wasn't fair after all he had done over there for them to judge him. He had answered the call of duty for his country. He had been brave, he didn't desert to Canada like a coward, he had saved lives, and he had volunteered to go bring home each and every American man lying in pieces at Mary Ann. These men were their brothers and sons and husbands, friends and dads. He did his best to respect, honor, and serve his brothers in arms. He didn't deserve these people's glares, or their spit and he resented them for it. A welcome home would've been nice. A pat on the back or a thank you from the American people would've meant so much. Unfortunately, that never came.

Chapter Nine

PEACE, LOVE, AND FREEDOM!

When Mike and Shirley got to Ohio, they were swept up in a whirlwind of activities preparing for their big day. One hundred people were coming to see them tie the knot, and there was lots of baking, sewing, and rehearsing to be done. Mike's mom and stepdad were driving up from Florida, and his brother, Terry, was flying in a few days before the ceremony. Terry's wife, Gertrude, stayed home to take care of their two young daughters, Terri Lee and Michelle. When all was said and done, Mike ended up having a grand total of three guests from his side of the family. The other one hundred ninety-seven people were there to see Shirley. They were folks from her little town that mostly knew Shirley's family from church, and the rest were extended relatives Shirley hadn't seen in ages.

PEACE, LOVE, AND FREEDOM!

In the days leading up to the wedding, Mike and Shirley had to meet with the priest for premarital counseling at the Catholic church Shirley's mom attended. It was not the church Shirley grew up in, and she no longer considered herself to be Catholic, but she knew it was important to her mom, so they decided to have a Catholic service. During the counseling, they were told that Mike and his family members would not be allowed to take communion because they had not been converted to Catholicism.

Being a new Christian, Shirley vehemently questioned the priest on these issues. She wanted to know why in the world that mattered. What difference did it make whether or not Mike was Catholic? The priest seemed to agree with her on many of the issues she had so boldly brought up to him about Catholicism during their counseling sessions. He didn't have a good answer for why Mike couldn't take communion, other than the fact that Catholic law said he couldn't. Shirley thought the priest seemed to be struggling with his own faith. He did allow them to choose their own set of vows from a few options and they eventually just decided to go with the flow. Have the Catholic service as it was supposed to be and make the family happy. Shirley's family was heavily Catholic.

The service was long and drawn out, in true Catholic fashion, beginning at ten in the morning and ending sometime after lunch. Shirley allowed her father to walk her down the aisle, continuing to keep the appearance of normalcy for the sake of her family. She had not shared any of her childhood abuse stories with Mike and really didn't want to dredge it all up again. She was moving past it in forgiveness and didn't think she needed to keep on telling people about it.

The whole congregation, minus the groom and his few guests, were given the holy communion. The ceremony had lasted so long, that as Mike and Shirley were on their way to the reception, they made a quick detour to grab a burger at Frish's Big Boy restaurant. They parked the green Triumph convertible Shirley's brother had given them as a surprise wedding gift. It was festively fashioned with newlywed garb flying in the wind and dragging behind the trunk. When they went inside to order, wearing the suit and wedding dress, all eyes were on them. Mike ordered a big boy burger, they sat down at a table and took their sweet time enjoying their first meal as husband and wife. The stares and smiles they got from other patrons only added to the fun.

The reception was held in the backyard of Shirley's childhood house. The whole family had pitched in, bringing covered dishes and preparing all of the food at their homes. They set up tables and chairs and enjoyed the time celebrating together, family barbeque style.

PEACE, LOVE, AND FREEDOM!

Mr. and Mrs. Michael and Shirley Hensley on their wedding day; July 3, 1971.

After the reception Mike and Shirley drove to a hotel not far from her parents' house and were disappointed to find that Mike's mom and stepdad were staying in the room right next door to theirs. At one point, Mike's mom knocked on their door to ask if they wanted to play cards. They declined. It was bad enough that their honeymoon plans were to stay with his mom and stepdad in Ft. Lauderdale, Florida, but to have them next door on their wedding night also, it was too much.

Mike's relationship with his mom and stepdad hadn't changed much since he returned from war, on the surface. In his heart, though, he fully belonged to his bride. She was his top priority and the one who gave him a sense of self-worth. He no longer needed to be affirmed by his mom and the sheriff.

The next day, the two couples headed down to Florida, and while Mike's mom and stepdad went straight through, Mike and Shirley decided to stop half way to break up the trip. This would give them a nice night of true privacy and a fun day in the mountains exploring together. They ended up stopping just north of Atlanta, Georgia and they both thought it was incredibly beautiful. They had heard of a really great waterfall near the end of the Appalachian Trail called Amicalola Falls.

When they arrived at the falls, Mike suggested they hike to the top. The water was rushing down, the sound of it spurring them on to explore nature and become one with the outdoors. There were no walkways or stairs leading to the top, over 700 feet tall. But Mike and Shirley were young and ambitious and they wanted to see it from the top. They made a plan with their eyes and began their ascent. It ended up being a lot of hard work, not only physically, but for their new marriage. Every time things got tricky, Shirley reminded Mike that it was his idea to climb up there, that she thought it was a better view of the falls from the ground anyway. Mike would get frustrated with poorly placed roots and footholds, angry that it wasn't easier for him and his new bride. Though they argued some on their way up, they also encouraged each other to keep going. Just as they reached the top, feeling relieved and happy again, Shirley's booney hat from Vietnam got caught up in the wind and went flying over the falls, out of sight.

They both paused for a moment in silence and peered down from where they had just climbed desperately searching for the hat, but they both knew they'd never see it again. Shirley sat down at the top of the falls, defeated. After the hard 730 foot climb, losing her hat from Vietnam was devastating. She didn't even know how much it had meant to her until it was gone. She had worn it all the time in the war. It went with her to the orphanage and to Cù Lao Ré island, to Da Nang and to their little inlet by the sea. She already missed it so badly and even though she knew it was silly, she began to cry over her lost hat.

When Mike saw how upsetting it was to her, his heart broke and he just wanted to get it back for her. When he finally resolved in his mind that it was gone, he cried too. He understood the significance of that hat to her. It had been a piece of her that understood what she had been through, and now it was gone. He comforted her and hugged her, and together they made their way back down to the car and drove to Florida.

They spent their three weeks in Florida going back and forth between Ft. Lauderdale, where they were living with Mike's mom and stepdad, and St. Petersburg, where Terry and Gert lived with their two little girls. They enjoyed spending most of their time in St. Pete and began talking with one another about moving there after they got out of the service. Coming from the childhoods they came from, they absolutely loved feeling like they belonged to a good family. Terry, his wife and kids, gave them both a feeling of new beginnings, of building a new family that loved each other well and were close. It was exactly what they wanted and they both dreamed of creating their own family, adding to the number of Hensleys. The new Hensleys, the ones where Terry and Mike would be the family patriarchs, where their kids would be cousins who were involved in each other's lives and where they'd all love each other and enjoy being together.

They made their way to Atlanta after their three-week honeymoon, and began their next year of service. Shirley found a nursing job at the hospital, and Mike served his last year as a surgical tech, stateside. Compared to his wartime duties, his job in the states almost felt like a breeze. Because of his experience, he was calm, collected, and still great at his job, far more comfortable than his counterparts who had only ever known the inside of a stateside hospital during peacetime. Take someone like Mike, put him in a quonset hut hospital, halfway around the world, in the middle of a war, and watch what happens to the person's skills. He was refined, like he'd been doing the job for decades.

Around the holiday season, they found a brand new International Harvester Scout, in a pretty sky blue for sale and convinced the car salesman to take a chance on giving them a loan, even though they had no credit. Mike argued that they had just come home from Vietnam, were newly married, and hadn't even had a chance to earn credit.

The car salesman liked them and respected that they had served in Vietnam. He went to the dealer and vouched for them to get a loan. They made the deal, traded in the Triumph, and even became friends with the car salesman. He was even invited over for their first Thanksgiving dinner in their little city apartment.

They enjoyed their year in Atlanta, spending some of their weekends driving up to the Blue Ridge mountains and finding good places to hike and get into nature. As they drove by the beautiful log cabins, Shirley started dreaming out loud about having a mountain cabin of their own one day. It was something to work toward, a dream they could share together and talk about when they imagined themselves in their old age. They could rock on the porch, sip on coffee and look out at these mountains they loved.

When Mike's year was complete, the Army tried awfully hard to keep him signed on. They offered promotions, pay raises, and more benefits if he'd re-up his contract for another term of service. The Hensleys thought about it but eventually decided they wanted to be free. Free to live where they wanted to live and do what they wanted to do. Mike didn't want to make a career out of the

Army, and he felt that if he stayed this time, it would be even harder to leave the next time. He felt grateful that he had served his country but he knew the time was right to be the owner of his life again.

They made their way down to St. Petersburg after being discharged, and asked Terry and Gert if they would keep their stuff for a couple months while they drove across the country, visiting the national parks. They were ready to do something fun and adventurous together that didn't involve being in the military. Shirley hadn't been hired anywhere yet in Florida and Mike wouldn't be starting medical school until the fall semester, so they reasoned that it was the perfect time to go exploring the country.

Right away, Shirley got to work sewing red curtains with white stars on them for the back windows, down both sides and across the rear, since they'd be living out of the car most of the time. They looked at that vehicle in all her patriotic glory and decided to name her Freedom. They didn't have the money to book hotels and planned to rely on campground bathrooms for showers here and there along the way. They had a Sears double sleeping bag they laid across the back of Freedom, a Coleman camping stove, and a small tent to set up when they made it to campgrounds. They had everything they needed. By May, they were off!

They drove from St. Pete to Cincinnati for the start of their great American road trip. They started off by visiting

PEACE, LOVE, AND FREEDOM!

family, first Shirley's and then Mike's grandmother in Illinois. Freedom was running well on gas that cost them 33 cents per gallon, and the young couple had nothing but time. They just planned to live off savings and travel the country together, celebrating the end of their military service. After their visits with family, they headed out west. Their first stop was in Iowa with a goal of making it through Colorado and after that, they hoped to see the Grand Canyon. Maybe they'd even make it over to California at some point. Having no real plans was the whole idea.

Having left so early in the year, many of the state parks were not open yet, especially the further north they traveled. They could get to the campgrounds to pitch their tent, but no facilities were available until after Memorial Day. There was one such stretch where they went an entire week without having a shower. When they were finally able to find one that was open in Estes Park, Colorado, they set up camp and decided to stay there for at least a few nights. Having made it to Colorado, they weren't in any hurry to move on anyway. This was the one of the destinations they were most looking forward to, and they wanted to see it all, the whole state. The four corners, Pike's Peak, Garden of the Gods, the Colorado National Monument, and Pueblo to see the Mesa Verde.

One afternoon while camping in one of the parks, they decided to grab their travel fishing poles and try to catch dinner from a nearby pond in the forest. Donning their usual camping garb, cut off denim shorts, cotton tees, and their booney hats—Shirley had bought a new one—they were off to the pond. They brought their small camping grill, knives, and butter and planned to fillet and grill their catch right out of the water.

Shirley set out the picnic blanket at the pond's edge, and Mike threw in his line, watching as several trout swam by. They both held their breath as a large trout came close, nearly eighteen inches long. Mike watched several times as the grandfather fish, they had nicknamed it, made his routine circles in the water, swimming out a few yards and then coming within inches of the bank. Over and over, it came by, never interested in the bait.

As the afternoon dragged on, Shirley gave up hope that they'd have fresh fish for dinner, and decided to lie down for a rest on the blanket. The next thing she knew, she heard a loud grunt from Mike and turned to see him leap into the pond with his big buck knife. He swiftly stabbed the knife into the water, impaled the grandfather trout through its side and launched it onto the shore. He then jumped back on the shore, finished killing dinner, and gave Shirley a smile that asked if she was impressed.

The whole thing happened so fast, she didn't even have time to say anything during the entire ordeal. She was in shock and impressed all at the same time and through giggles asked him if he was a descendant of Davy Crockett.

Mike was satisfied with that response, and set to work filleting the beast. He felt like a pioneer, proud to have secured food for his woman off the land. They both agreed, fresh fish had never tasted so good.

At another point during the roadtrip, they got one of the biggest scares of their lives as they were driving down a stretch of remote road in the desert. Freedom was the only car on the road, and Mike and Shirley had been enjoying the thrill of being off the beaten path. They were listening to America, "A Horse with No Name," had the windows down, and Shirley's feet were on the dashboard, when Mike noticed something disturbing pop into his rearview mirror. As if out of nowhere, a gang of about two hundred motorcycles were quickly approaching behind them.

Mike didn't know what to do. His thoughts raced. He had his brand new wife in the car, they were alone in the desert, and the motorcycles would be on top of them any second. Shirley sat up, they had closed the windows, and shut the radio off. She said a silent prayer that nothing bad would happen.

As the first few motorcycles reached the car, they slowed down a bit, but then whipped right around them. The rest of the gang followed suit and not one touched the car. Mike just kept driving at the same steady speed and kept his eyes on the road. As the men passed by, he could read the back of their leather jackets—they were Hell's Angels. A motorcycle gang with a reputation for being outlaws and considered an organized crime syndicate by the US Justice Department.

Mike and Shirley stayed calm, tried not to stare at them as they filed by and kept sending silent prayers up to God. As the last of the Hell's Angels made his way around the vehicle and out of sight ahead, Mike pulled over so he could catch his breath, realizing for the first time that he had been holding it the whole time. They let time put more distance between them and the Hell's Angels and then continued on their great American road trip.

With another week down, it came time for them to make their once weekly phone call home to let everyone know where they were, how they were doing, and check on the family. Then off to the Grand Canyon the next day!

They found a payphone at a gas station on their way to Arizona and inserted the coins. Terry answered the phone and Mike could tell immediately that something was wrong. Terry filled Mike in on what had happened over the past week. Their mother, Helen, had become very ill and was in the ICU. She was being prepped for surgery on one of her lungs to remove a lump that had been found. Since she was a smoker, the family was all worried that it might be cancerous. The procedure would take place the next morning. Shirley stood nearby trying to hear both sides of the conversation, sensing the urgency in Terry's voice, and rubbing Mike's arm gently as she understood the situation.

PEACE, LOVE, AND FREEDOM!

Mike hung up the phone, looked at Shirley with disappointment in his eyes, and without much conversation, they both knew their trip had ended. They'd head back to Florida first thing in the morning and go straight to the hospital. It was an abrupt and stressful end to what was supposed to be their time of peace together on the road. Free as birds, happy as clams. It was over with one phone call.

Shirley knew the kind of relationship Mike had with his mom, and she understood how much he loved her and wanted her love and attention in return. Though he tried very hard not to need his mother's approval anymore, this news hit him hard, like a slap in the face . . . he still needed her to love him.

Shirley watched in silence as he drove them home, anxious, sad, and worried, and she hoped his mother would be alright at least until they arrived. Shirley prayed that if she was alright, that she'd appreciate the fact that her son had dropped everything to come to her. Though her trip to Paris was more important than taking Mike to the induction center as he left for the Army, just a boy, he never held it against her. Though he always felt like the third wheel in her new life with the sheriff, he was always there for her.

Shirley sure hoped she'd validate him, that she'd tell him she loved him, that he was a good son, that she was proud of him and missed him, and wished she had spent more time with him when he was growing up. All of these thoughts swirled around behind her eyes, as she looked at him, driving fast, face tense, not knowing exactly how to handle his emotions.

They briefly talked about their disappointment in not getting to see the Grand Canyon, but they consoled themselves with the idea that they'd be back. One day they'd travel like this again. One day they'd see the Grand Canyon. One day....

Helen was fine after her surgery. The mass was not cancerous and she lived a long life, staying involved with her sons and their families. In her later years, she became known as the beloved "Grammy Jo" to all five grandchildren, spending Christmases together and making up for lost time with her sons.

Chapter Ten

BACK TO THE WORLD

Shirley and Mike both found entry level jobs in St. Pete and though their job titles and places of employment changed a few times over the years, they continued to serve their fellow Americans throughout the rest of their careers.

In the meantime, Mike had started taking his college courses, still planning to become a doctor, but after a few weeks of being in class with a bunch of greenies, whining and complaining about simple things and not knowing basic medical skills, he couldn't handle it. After what he had seen and done in the war, trying to learn amongst kids who had just graduated high school a few months back was extremely frustrating to him. He told Shirley he couldn't do it anymore and quit school before the first semester had ended. The other kids knew nothing. They knew nothing of pain or death, of surgery or what it's like to try to save lives or to lose lives. He couldn't be around it, not one more day.

Shirley understood. They didn't need to discuss it any further, she just knew how he felt and she didn't expect him to get over it. War was real for them, and being around people who had no idea what it is like, was tough. Shirley knew that Mike was highly intelligent and would find something else to pour his life into. She wasn't worried about it and Mike was so grateful to have a wife who understood. A partner that he didn't have to explain himself to any further. They were there together, working the war, and it gave them a silent bond, a quiet understanding and a mutual respect for each other's pain.

Shirley started working at St. Anthony's hospital as a nurse on the cardiac telemetry floor and Mike decided, against all warnings from his brother, to follow in Terry's footsteps and attend the police academy. There, he met a friend named John. John was a very likeable guy, funny, smart, and enjoyable to be around. He and Mike hit it off great right from the start, and even began carpooling to classes. John was married to Gayle and had a front license tag that read, "John & Gayle" with a heart around it. The other guys started to pick up on how close Mike and John were, and saw that they arrived in the John & Gayle car every day. It wasn't long before that became their nicknames, John was still John, and Mike was now Gayle.

BACK TO THE WORLD

By March of 1973, Mike and John joined the St. Pete Police department together, and Shirley was becoming more established at the hospital. Feeling as though they both had good, steady jobs, they started searching for their first house. Having children was becoming the topic of conversation more often and they both thought they should be out of the apartment before becoming parents.

After about a week of house hunting they decided on a two bedroom, one bathroom house in a quiet neighborhood. It was small, but it had a pretty big yard that they could picture their future children running around in one day. They had no money to fill it with furniture, so they made do with their two bean bag chairs, a dining table made out of a large wooden spool, and the red, white, and blue bedroom set they had purchased for the apartment. It wasn't much to start out with, but it was enough. The house was $32,000 dollars, with a monthly payment of $140 including taxes and insurance. That payment scared Mike half to death. He knew from the time he signed those papers, for the rest of his life, he would have to be a responsible man. A man who worked hard and provided for his family.

At the same time, now that they were making a little bit of money, they thought about buying their first grown up toy. They were so close to the water, and Mike worked the area by the pier, near the marina. During his patrols, he always noticed all the sailboats in the water. It looked like a dream. He started talking to the other officers about what kinds of sailboats they had, how to get a boat slip at the marina, and he convinced Shirley to attend a couple of boat shows in the area, just to look.

A short time later, a boat slip became available to Mike, a perk of being one of the city's protectors. Usually people had to wait a long time for one to become available, but someone in the department had heard Mike was interested and decided it was time to sell his slip. Mike snatched it right up, without even having a boat. Within a few weeks time, Mike and Shirley had found a small, used sailboat. It was a nineteen foot, Alberg Typhoon with a cuddy cabin.

Neither one of them knew how to sail, but they took it out anyway, determined to learn as they went along. It had two sails, a full keel and outboard motor. They learned quickly and it wasn't long before they were heeling through the bay, standing atop one handrail, holding the sails, while the other rail skimmed the water, the boat leaning on it's side, whipping through the wind. They loved that boat. How relaxing it was to hear nothing but the wind in the sails and the water slapping the walls. They named her the Silent Runner.

Mike and John continued to hang out and Shirley became friends with Gayle. The four of them would go on double dates together, but before they could even make it to the restaurant or the movies, John and Mike were pulling over to bust criminals, and would even have the women call into the station for police to come while the men were detaining the perpetrators. Shirley and Gayle just came to expect that they'd have a stop or two of police work to get through before actually getting to dinner. At that time, fresh out of the academy, Mike and John still thought they were going to save the city. Catch every bad guy, shut down all the illegal activity, and protect every citizen. It didn't matter to them if they were on duty or not, they were young and idealistic, and the law was in their blood.

Within the year, they found out Shirley was pregnant with their first child! John and Gayle also found out they were expecting at the same time. It was all very exciting and the couples did everything together, even attending lamaze classes at the hospital with each other.

By this time, Shirley had worked her way up to the Charge Nurse for the cardiac telemetry floor and was busy managing other nurses and making rounds with doctors. While she really enjoyed the actual bedside jobs, connecting and caring for the patients, being the charge nurse while pregnant worked out nicely for her. She continued to work at St. Anthony's until the baby was born. She delivered at the same hospital, a beautiful, healthy, and perfect baby girl. They named her Heather.

Shirley stayed home to take care of Heather, and Mike continued to make a name for himself within the police department. Walking Heather around the neighborhood in the stroller, Shirley began to meet new people. On one such walk, she met her neighbor from a couple doors down the street, Ruth, who invited Shirley to come to a Bible study at the church on their same street. Thrilled to have made a friend and to be invited to a church, Shirley went to the very next meeting, bringing Heather along. For the first time in her spiritual life, she felt like she was exactly where she needed to be, it just resonated with her soul in a way she had never experienced at any other church.

She went to that little church at the end of the street every Sunday. At one Bible study meeting, Mike had come in to tell her he was headed to work, in his police uniform. A sweet older woman, the pastor's wife, fell in love with him immediately. A handsome young man in uniform, with his precious young wife and brand new baby daughter. They all thought he was just the sweetest young man.

When asked about his spiritual beliefs, Shirley told them she was praying for him every day to give his life to God. From that point on, everyone else was praying for him too. The pastor's wife was also the director of the choir, and she had them all praying for the young man in uniform, officer Mike Hensley. His charm and warm personality were just as effective as ever, and the people of that church desperately wanted to see him choose to live his life for Christ.

BACK TO THE WORLD

Ruth's husband, Carl, even became best friends with Mike, and over the course of time, the two couples became inseparable. Mike and Carl would go out fishing together and have deep discussions and debates about the Bible and God. Mike wasn't sure that Christianity wasn't more of a crutch for people than actual truth, and Carl would patiently listen and give his thoughts about all of Mike's hang ups, all while maintaining their close friendship. After some of their lengthy discussions about having faith, Mike would turn to Shirley and ask her if she believed everything Carl had been saying. She would respond simply in the affirmative. She believed everything he was saying. That always made Mike stop and think about it a little longer before just dismissing it. And Shirley was so thankful for Carl, because as a new Christian herself, she didn't have the biblical knowledge and theology that Carl was bringing to the conversations, but she was sure glad he was comfortable talking about it all.

By this time, Mike had begun to get more and more involved with his police buddies in his personal life, trying hard to fit in and be accepted into their brotherhood. He was a rookie cop, trying to impress his training officer, who he saw as god, and this meant he began staying out late at night. After their shifts were over, around two-thirty in the morning, instead of going home, they'd go straight to Mike's Happy Tap, the local cop bar, and have a few drinks together. He was working undercover at the time, growing his hair out long and smoking just as much as ever.

He didn't really see the big deal Shirley made when he would come home so late smelling like alcohol and cigarettes. He wanted her to understand that to build his career, he would need to fit into this subculture of being a law enforcement officer. They worked hard and they played hard, they were tough guys, they did what they wanted to do, and they didn't need any help from anybody about how to live their lives. This is where Mike began to find his identity.

Shirley decided to let it go on the surface; she didn't want to have arguments with Mike when they were together. Instead, she launched her own silent battle against these behaviors in her heart. She prayed for Mike even harder. She prayed diligently for him to come to know Jesus Christ in a personal way. She knew that when he came to know Jesus, in a real, self-chosen way, his behaviors would change. So she prayed continuously for her husband.

Mike was surrounded by Christians outside of work and he started to notice the difference in how he felt being around his friends and family, and around his work buddies. The bar became less attractive after work, and as he heard more about getting his approval and value from God rather than his training officers, he began to care less what they thought of his personal decisions to go home and be with his family. Shirley was starting to notice the change in him too and prayed all the more.

As they were sitting in the pews of the church one Sunday morning, listening to a sermon about God's grace, forgiveness, and promises through the person of Jesus Christ, the pastor asked if anyone would like to commit their life to Christ. He asked those people to come forward as the choir began to sing. Shirley sat with Heather on her knee, speaking to God in her heart.

As the choir watched, Mike slowly got up from his seat and walked down the aisle, all the way forward. He knelt down and prayed to be made into a new man. The church members, who had all been praying for this very thing for months, each celebrated in their own ways. Some broke into big smiles, some cried tears of happiness, and some went over to hug him and congratulate him after the service. He had taken a big step toward faith in his life, and the people who loved him most, couldn't be happier for him.

Feeling the weight of being a new dad, not knowing how to be a good dad and not having grown up with a good example of fatherhood, Mike felt like he needed help. He wanted a roadmap for his life, something to guide him into being a good father for his baby girl, a year old now, and a good husband to Shirley for their whole lives. He thought Jesus sounded like the best roadmap for life he had ever come across, and he was ready to jump in with both feet.

Chapter Eleven

COUNTRY BOUND

Life went on, with Mike focusing more on building his career through hard work and integrity and less through impressing or fitting in with the guys. He was spending more time with his family and friends and was digging deeper into what it meant to be a Christian man, and to live his life in a way that pleased God. The more he looked around at seasoned cops, living the typical way many cops do, he wasn't impressed anymore with their drinking and staying away from their families. The closer he looked, the more he realized that he didn't want to be anything like that. He wanted to be a family man, an honest man, and a man of faith.

Mike and Terry had made contact with their dad again, living in Reno, Nevada. He wasn't very healthy, but the sons had both convinced him to move to St. Pete so they could help take care of him. He could be around his granddaughters, Terri Lee, Michelle, and Heather and live the rest of his days around family. Edward agreed to move to Florida and was set to make the move in a couple months time. Mike was looking forward to seeing his dad again, and now that he was a Christian man, he thought he'd be better able to forgive his dad for being an alcoholic while they grew up and maybe try to have a better relationship with him.

Unfortunately, weeks before Edward was scheduled to move, he found himself at the veteran's hospital in San Francisco, California. With this news, Mike feared his father would never make it back to Florida, never meet his granddaughters. Shortly after being admitted, Edward died of his illnesses at the age of 61. Mike and Terry arranged for his funeral to be held at Woodlawn Memorial Gardens in Norfolk, Virginia. With their father being a WWII veteran, the Hensley brothers wanted him resting in a place known for honoring veterans. They both flew up for the service and said their final goodbyes.

By 1975, Mike was awarded Officer of the Quarter for the St. Petersburg Police Department's fourth quarter award. It felt great to be recognized for excellence so early in his career. He had been working hard to learn about criminal justice, and he and John were attending school together at the junior college to earn their two-year degrees. Mike was able to use his G.I. bill to pay for school, attending classes at night, while still juggling his full time police career.

Shirley became pregnant with their second child, another girl, due in the summer of 1976. They welcomed their second baby girl into the world in July and named her Holly. Shirley decided to stay home for another couple of years to take care of the girls while they were so young.

Over the next few years, Mike continued to attend night classes, transferring to the University of South Florida after having earned his associate's degree. At USF, he majored in criminal justice and graduated in 1980, while continuing his full time police career. He even worked off-duty jobs to make a little extra cash for the family. His job, coupled with seven years of going to school part time, had been all consuming. He was seen as an excellent officer who had a promising future with the department. He had already been promoted to detective and he had even won the Ned March Award for outstanding work solving burglaries. It was a great honor to be recognized again, but it was all beginning to take its toll. He absolutely loved the work, but it was a lot to deal with, a heavy-hearted career that could crush his spirits in an instant. Some days were good and other days were completely disheartening.

When the Hensleys found out that their best friends, Carl and Ruth, were leaving St. Pete to move out to the country, roughly an hour away, the news was devastating. They had also had a baby in 1976 and were pregnant again.

Mike and Shirley really believed that they'd all raise their children together and be best friends forever. They were a part of each other's daily lives and the thought of losing them to another city was too much. Carl had taken a job to run a Christian youth camp in Brooksville, Florida called Lakewood Retreat. They'd be gone by the end of the year.

Mike and Shirley talked long and hard about their future. Did they really want to put down permanent roots in St. Pete? There was so much crime, as Mike knew all too well, and the girls were getting older and ready for school. Not to mention that without their friends, they felt lost. By the end of 1980, the Hensleys had decided that it was more important to raise their kids in the country and with friends who felt like family than it was to keep putting deeper and deeper roots down in a place where they didn't want their kids to grow up. Carl and Ruth were thrilled to be reunited with their best friends, and they were able to get a job lined up for both Mike and Shirley at their Christian camp. In 1981, the Hensleys left St. Petersburg for good and moved to Brooksville with their friends. Mike knew he needed a break from the heart-wrenching police work he had been doing and they both looked forward to the wide open spaces of the country and a slower pace of life.

In his eight years with the St. Petersburg Police Department, Mike had worked many positions and wore several titles. In his early undercover days, working with the ABARS unit (Armed Burglary And Robbery) he played a drunk decoy, almost getting stabbed in the back by a robber one night. He laid on the pavement pretending to be lethargic in one of St. Pete's most crime ridden pockets of town. The robber stood over Mike, riffling through his pockets, looking for his wallet. He had his knife in hand in case he needed to use it on the drunk fool. Mike's team looked on from a distance as the man roughed him up a bit, trying to locate the wallet.

When he finally got his hands on it, batting away Mike's weak attempts to protect it, he emptied it of its cash, signaling the team to move in and take the criminal down. When they found the knife he had, too small for them to have seen at a distance, they were all glad he hadn't been more aggressive with Mike from the start. There had been numerous injuries and even some murders of drunkards who had been robbed in the streets. Mike had been lucky.

Later in his career, once he became a detective, he worked a high stakes and high intensity child kidnapping. A man had picked up a young girl whom he used to foster from her home and had taken her into the woods. His plan was to bury her in a deep hole to make her pay for telling the authorities about the abuse she endured under his care. Terry, Mike, and their teams had tracked him to the location. and as they closed in around him, the man became irate. He began screaming that he was going to shoot them all and the girl too if they came any closer.

Several policemen sneaked around the sides to flank the man, and when he realized how close they were, he opened fire, shooting one policeman right in his chest. The other officers moved in quickly and subdued the kidnapper. Mike ran over and grabbed the little girl under her arms, yanking her out of the hole and carrying her away from the commotion as fast as he could. When the girl realized she was rescued, she began sobbing and hugging Mike tightly. Luckily, the police officer who had been shot had been wearing a bulletproof vest, which saved his life, and no other officers were injured. Mike went home that night and kissed his wife and hugged his daughters for a long time. Any time children were involved in his work, it always took a different kind of toll on the men.

Switching from law enforcement to full time ministry was a difficult change for Mike. He went from being a promising detective, involved in some of the city's most important cases, to working as the maintenance man at a youth camp. Fixing broken water pipes, mending fences, replacing worn out sports equipment—it was a big change of pace. Shirley was working in the cafeteria, cooking all day long, providing delicious meals for campers. With Shirley in the kitchen, Lakewood Retreat gained a reputation for being a camp that actually served good food.

The Hensley girls were having fun living at a youth camp. They had learned all of the shortcuts, mastered all of the games, and felt like they ruled the place. They had free rein of the land, and after having lived in their tiny St. Pete house, it felt good to be able to go run around outside without their parents' supervision. The camp was large, with a big lake, a petting zoo, a community pool, the cafeteria, a game and snack shack, and plenty of outdoor spaces to run wild. During this time, the Hensley sisters became best friends with Ruth and Carl's oldest child, Josh. The three of them would find all sorts of ways to have fun and occasionally cause trouble for their parents. It was a fantastic time in the lives of the kids.

As the time went on and they started to approach the one year anniversary of working at the camp, Mike and Shirley began discussing a career change yet again. They had become used to the slower pace of life and couldn't imagine moving back to the city, but they weren't sure that full time ministry was what they were supposed to be doing with their lives. They had spent years training and equipping themselves to serve others in a different way. Shirley was a very skilled nurse, and while she was also a very skilled cook, she knew she had spent a lot of time in school, in the war, and at the hospitals, honing specialty skills. She was trained to be a nurse and felt a responsibility that if she was going to be working, she should be putting all that education and experience to good use. And Mike missed his law enforcement days, when he really felt as though he was making a big difference in his community. They knew working at the camp was important, but it wasn't fulfilling their call to serve others like they thought it would.

They prayed about the decision and ultimately felt as though they were to return to the work they knew best. It was a wonderful realization for them, that they didn't have to be doing full time ministry to serve God, that they could also serve Him in their regular careers. After their first year at Lakewood, they began looking for new jobs.

In the meantime, they came into contact with a Canadian woman who was a beekeeper, lived in the woods near Lakewood, and owned quite a bit of property. She was looking to sell some of it, and she immediately took a liking to Mike and Shirley and their young family. She wanted them to be able to raise their kids on some property where they would have room to run around. She told Mike to pick out any piece he wanted from her land. It was unbelievable! They picked out a two and half acre lot on a gorgeous piece of wooded land. The county added a road for them to access their property, and the Hensleys got to name it. Mike knew right away, he wanted it to be called Shirley Drive. Eventually more plots of land were sold and others came to live on Shirley drive, each with their own acreage and woods. It was beautiful and the

COUNTRY BOUND

Hensley's loved the idea of giving their kids a wholesome, country upbringing.

They built a three-bedroom house with a front porch and a stone fireplace. They modeled much of it after the mountain cabins of North Georgia they loved so much. It had a cabin-like feel to it, which had much to do with their choice of warm woods and cozy mountain decor. They loved their little home in the country and lived there for 25 years raising their family and serving their community.

Chapter Twelve

MISSION ACCOMPLISHED

Right around the time Mike and Shirley built their home in Brooksville, Carl and Ruth decided to start their own church. They enlisted the help of friends, like Mike and Shirley, as well as some others, and they started meeting on Sundays for church. They called it Community Bible Church (CBC) and Carl was the pastor. The church picked up more and more popularity as they grew in numbers and moved into larger spaces to accommodate all of the families joining in on Sundays. Eventually Mike started teaching Sunday school to the adults after the main service and things were going well. Their best friends were the leaders and they were helping to build something that served people in their community. They felt a high sense of purpose and fulfillment at CBC.

MISSION ACCOMPLISHED

Wanting to make a difference in their new small town, Mike decided to apply to the sheriff's office of Hernando County. He knew he'd be starting his law enforcement career over from the beginning, but the Hensleys were confident that Brooksville was the place to plant their roots. They had moved quite a bit since the war, but they weren't planning on moving again. Brooksville was their home.

The new sheriff of the department was trying to turn it around by hiring more educated and experienced guys. Mike immediately got hired on as a deputy, and as one of the only guys at HCSO with a college degree, he felt like he was stepping back in time. He had to buy his own belt and equipment, his police car looked like it was going to break down any day, and the office was located inside an old, somewhat dilapidated house in the center of town. He had no partner, no back up, and didn't necessarily trust the other guys in the department. They had a very southern, good ol' boy mentality when it came to things like black crimes versus white crimes, the Brooksville chapter of the KKK (Ku Klux Klan), and Mike wasn't so sure that some of them weren't actually involved with such backward thinking hate groups.

It was very primitive compared to what he was used to in St. Pete. The public seemed primitive, the police seemed just as so, and it seemed as though they were all related to one another, or had attended school together since they were five. Everyone knew everyone and the police may have been a little too gung-ho about the power they held. If the sheriff liked a young man, he promoted him based on that alone. There was no training, no testing, it was all decided by the sheriff. It was a bit of culture shock, but Mike was determined to stick around and help make changes from within the department.

Mike was told that they couldn't offer to pay him very much but if he stuck around, the department would grow and become more advanced. It sounded good to Mike. He accepted the position with a whopping $13,000 a year salary and hoped to help the department grow into one with a good reputation and one deserving of respect. There were plenty of the same crimes in Brooksville that St. Pete had, like robbery, murder, and domestic violence. Only now Mike was answering calls on his own and back up would be 30 to 40 minutes away on the other side of the county. He also had his fair share of calls about cows being on the road, which he had never dealt with in the city. He had to pack his lunch and dinner, as there were no restaurants in the rural areas that he worked. It was a completely different kind of world than the one where he had learned how to be an officer.

Over the years, Mike saw more and more college-educated men being hired on, more men coming from bigger city departments, who had some valuable police experience to bring to the table, and the whole feel of it

MISSION ACCOMPLISHED

started to change. They moved into a new office, a bit more modern, and started requiring more training for their officers and more accountability. If there were any backwards cops left, they were slowly but surely weeding them out with new policies and procedures to make sure the officers were being held to a higher standard.

The sheriff promoted Mike and another officer named Richard into positions of more power, because he liked them, and it was there that Mike was able to help institute real change. He and Richard started the first testing the department had ever seen. No more promotions based on being well liked, the men had to learn and pass tests to get promoted. It wasn't a popular move at first, but over time, it came to be a widely respected procedure for moving up. It drew in more educated guys and got rid of the ones who couldn't cut it. It also helped the men feel more secure, that their future career was in their own hands and their ability to learn and be a good officer, not just dependent on whether the big man in charge liked them or not. It was a good period of growth for the Hernando County Sheriff's Department.

When Shirley quit cooking for the camp, she found a job at Lyke's Memorial Hospital in Brooksville. She worked part time on the medical surgery floor two or three days a week. Unfortunately, whenever Shirley left for a night shift at the hospital, it really upset Holly at home. She didn't want her mom leaving at night. Shirley decided it was more important for her daughter to have her mother at home during the evenings than it was to make good money. So she switched jobs to become the school nurse at the girls' elementary school, Eastside Elementary.

When Shirley talked to Mike about wanting to have a third child now that both girls were into their school years, Mike told her that they didn't really have enough money, and he wanted to focus on building his career back up. He was completely satisfied with having the two girls and didn't know if he wanted to have a baby again. They decided to put a third child on hold until Mike felt more stable in his career and got a promotion or two.

Over the following years, Mike's career took many different twists and turns. In the next election, the guy he had been supporting for sheriff lost, and the new sheriff demoted Mike as soon as he took office. With a pay cut and feeling like he was on the chopping block, talks of another child were off the table. But after only a few months, the sheriff promoted Mike to sergeant and made him the very first officer in charge of Internal Affairs.

HCSO had never had Internal Affairs before, but the sheriff knew it was badly needed for them to become a legitimate agency, and he really liked what he saw in Mike—an honest, loyal, and hardworking young man.

After that, Mike worked hard to continue making himself marketable for more promotions and for transferring, if need be. Every four years, when the election

MISSION ACCOMPLISHED

rolled around, he knew he could be canned and have to start over at a different department somewhere in the country. It was stressful thinking about taking care of his family around those times. Not wanting to have to uproot them and move for a new job, he did everything possible to make himself an asset to the agency.

By this time, Holly was in third grade, Heather would be in middle school in less than a year, and Shirley was entering her late thirties. She told Mike she really wanted to try to have another child. They talked about how nice it was to be out of the baby stage, but at the same time, Shirley felt that the family was not complete. It wouldn't have been Mike's first choice, but he loved his wife and his family and he trusted that God would let whatever was supposed to happen, happen.

They decided that they'd try to get pregnant for six months. If there wasn't a baby on the way by then, they would drop the subject. With Heather and with Holly, they got pregnant the first month they tried, but a decade later, things were different. Month after month passed with no pregnancy and Mike started to become settled into the idea that the family wouldn't be changing. He was more than fine with that. But Shirley prayed even harder, desperately wanting to have one more child. In the sixth month, just before they closed that door forever, she felt it. She knew it. She went to have a pregnancy test done at the clinic and it was positive!

When Mike came home from work that day, she told him out on the front porch, with a few butterflies in her stomach. Mike was completely taken off guard, having already allowed himself to believe it wasn't going to happen. After he got over his disbelief, he was genuinely happy. Happy that Shirley was happy, excited that their family would be blessed with another child. They went into the house to tell the girls the good news and when Mike told them the family would be adding a new member, little Holly's eyes grew wide with excitement and she asked if they were finally getting her that pet monkey she'd been dreaming about. She was a little disappointed to find out it was going to be a baby, but only a little.

From that point on, they all started wishing for a boy. With having had two girls already, and with Terry and Gert having had two girls as well, they started thinking about how this was the last chance for the Hensley name to be passed down to the next generation. They also thought it would be more fun to get back into all the baby stuff if it was different than before. They decided to be surprised at the hospital and in January of 1986 when the newest little Hensley came into the world screaming, the doctor yelled out that it was a boy. They named him Heath Michael.

With the family now complete, Mike thought it would be a good time to head back to school to earn his master's degree in criminal justice. The girls were busy with their

MISSION ACCOMPLISHED

school and activities, and Shirley was busy at home taking care of the new baby. Over the next several years, Mike worked his shift, and then took classes at night. He was continuously concerned with making himself a valuable employee, one worth keeping around, and he knew an advanced degree couldn't hurt his luck. He finished his program right around the time Heath turned five years old. Heather was just a year away from graduating high school and Holly was right behind her. To make a bit of extra money for upcoming graduations and college, Mike started teaching part time as an adjunct professor at Saint Leo College, while still working his normal shifts. He enjoyed teaching so much that he even began leading some officer training and professional development classes at work.

Shirley had been staying home to raise Heath, but when he started kindergarten, she was ready to start working again. She wanted something that would work out well with his schedule while he was still so young, so she could be home with him after school. She knew the only job that would allow her the time off she wanted was to return to being the school nurse. The pay wasn't very good and it wasn't exactly what she hoped to be doing with her skills, but it was what worked at the time, and so, that's what she did.

Around this time, the Hensleys faced one of the most difficult losses of relationship they would ever experience.

Too many differences between Carl and Mike led to hurtful words, which left a gaping hole in their friendship. The hole became unmendable as time passed and the wounds festered. After trying to return to Community Bible Church in the aftermath of the incident, the Hensleys felt uncomfortable and knew it was time to move on. Their long-time friendship with Carl and Ruth was over. It was a loss they mourned heavily, as Carl and Ruth had become like their own family. They wouldn't reconnect until the writing of this book, after 20 years of living separate lives in the same town.

When Mike and Shirley left CBC, they started attending a small, red-brick, country church just down the road from their house. It was called Spring Lake United Methodist Church (SLUMC) and was led by pastor David.

Mike and Shirley thought David was the most genuine and humble person they had ever met. They immediately hit it off with David and his wife, Sherry, and jumped into the church full force. Mike taught Sunday school with Shirley to the adults, he played guitar in the worship band, and they became very close with a group of friends whom they would spend the next decade of their lives with. It was a thriving little church, full of loving people, and open arms . . . it was a true picture of what they believed the church should look like. People there were authentic. They weren't perfect, and they didn't pretend to be. It was an amazing place to be and to raise Heath. They loved Spring

MISSION ACCOMPLISHED

Lake and they were well loved by the members there, many of whom are still great friends with the Hensleys to this day.

In 1992, Shirley started working for hospice. She had been dreaming about working for hospice for years, ever since she had seen those nurses come into the hospital with their patients. Shirley would chat with the hospice nurses and hoped that one day, that's what she'd be able to do. She got a job with Pasco Hernando Hospice, part time, to still be able to take care of Heath after school. She absolutely loved it! She felt like she was returning to what she got into nursing for in the first place: patient care. No more rushing in and out of patient rooms to set IVs and run to the next room to do something else. At hospice, the nurses were encouraged to spend time with their patients, go slow, get to know them and their family members. Shirley, being a lifelong nurse and having started the way she did, was very comfortable being around death. She had always seen it as a natural part of life, and it didn't bother her to be around it. In fact, she felt blessed to be the one helping people in their final moments, helping them let go and move on. To be able to help someone remain calm and go peacefully into their next life, while they trust her with their last words and with their legacy, is something she can hardly describe to those who have not experienced it. Shirley always loved patient care the most, and this was a perfect fit for her.

In 1995, Mike was selected to attend the FBI National Academy as a member of the 181st class. It is a ten-week long course in Quantico, Virginia where the chosen officers are put through strenuous physical tests and rigorous law enforcement classes, including forensics, terrorism, and behavioral sciences. Mike's roommate was a great guy, also named Mike, who was the chief of police from Traverse City Michigan. Mike really enjoyed getting to meet other leaders in law enforcement from around the country.

Over the ten weeks, they did daily physical training, lots of running and lifting weights, they attended classes and even had time to do some sightseeing in Washington D.C. It was a fantastic time for Mike, but even though he was having so much fun, he really missed Shirley and Heath at home. To make the ten weeks go by faster, they had planned four trips to see each other. Mike came home twice, and Shirley and Heath went up twice, one of the times being at the very end for Mike's graduation. Holly also flew in from nursing school to see her dad graduate. She had joined the army to become a nurse after high school, following in her mother's footsteps. When she got to Virginia, Mike invited her to join him on his final physical exam called, The Yellow Brick Road. It was a 10K obstacle course designed to put their months of physical training to the test. Holly was in incredible shape, being in the military herself, and they enjoyed the challenge

MISSION ACCOMPLISHED

together. Mike came back from the FBI National Academy at 44 years old and in the best shape of his life.

Eventually Mike became the Chief Sheriff of the Hernando County Sheriff Office. He held other titles throughout the years, like Detective, Sergeant, Lieutenant over the whole Criminal Investigation Division, and Major. He had a 27-year career with HCSO and was instrumental in bringing the department into modern operations. He was a beacon of change for Brooksville law enforcement, and having worked his way up from the bottom, a deputy in the old house, to the chief of a department with more than 400 well-educated and respectable deputies, his family was incredibly proud of his accomplishments. He retired in 2009 . . . for a couple of minutes.

When he left the sheriff's office, he was offered an enticing position as the head of the medical examiner's office HCSO worked with. He knew the doctor who owned the practice and she really wanted him to come and manage her doctors. The offer was too good to turn down. Great pay and flexible hours. He took the job. Besides, Shirley was still working with hospice, so it wasn't like they were completely retired yet anyway.

Shirley had been working as a hospice nurse since 1992, and really enjoyed her job. After 20 years with hospice, she retired in 2012 and Mike followed suit, retiring from the medical examiner's office in 2013. Altogether, starting from the time Mike served in the Army, to the St. Pete Police Department, to Lakewood Retreat, Hernando County Sheriff's Office and the District 5 Medical Examiner's Office, Mike served the people of his country and community for nearly 43 years.

From the Army, to St. Anthony's Hospital, to Lakewood Retreat, Lyke's Memorial Hospital, the Eastside Elementary School nurse, and Pasco Hernando Hospice Care Center, Shirley served the people of her country and community for nearly 35 years. If you throw in being an incredible mother, which certainly has served the country and community, the number rises to 43 years.

EPILOGUE

Nearly 40 years later, Mike and Shirley made it to the Grand Canyon. They stood together, overlooking the red and brown ravine, arms wrapped tightly around one another while they took in all that it meant to finally be standing there. A lifetime had passed since they had been so close and now they were there, on the edge of the magnificent grand canyon, sharing it with their youngest son on his 25th birthday.

In the years following the Vietnam War and their military service, Mike and Shirley settled down in St. Petersburg, Florida and joined Terry and Gert in bringing forth a new era of Hensleys. They each began building a family that would give the Hensley name a totally revived meaning, a family name that stood for belonging and a love for one another that is fierce and unconditional. It's a true gift to each member who gets to proudly wear the Hensley name, either until marriage or because of it. Hensley's belong, no matter how they come to be part of this incredible family.

Between 1974 and 1986, Mike and Shirley welcomed three children into their family. Heather, Holly, and Heath. Their three children are all married and have families of their own. They currently have thirteen grandchildren! Heather married Don and together they have four children: Casey, Cameron, and twins Samuel and Savannah. Holly married high school sweetheart Chris, and together they have six children: Elizabeth, Caleb, Joshua, Nathan, Isaac, and Abigail. And Heath married his middle school sweetheart, Terah. Together we have three children: Solomon, Elijah, and Anna Kay.

Today Mike and Shirley enjoy spending time at their retirement cabin in the Blue Ridge Mountains. They host friends and family on an almost weekly basis and they are finally getting to travel around the country and the world the way they always dreamed they would.

In 2015, Mike and Shirley returned to Vietnam to face their pasts and find healing from the wounds their souls still carried. They visited the orphanage where they met and the cliffs where they used to watch the Hueys come in and dream about their futures together. It was there, where it all began, that they were really able to look back and see clearly that they had accomplished their mission. They had indeed created a life of peace together. . . .

EPILOGUE

Top: A note Mike wrote to Shirley in Vietnam, 1970.
Bottom Left: Sitting on their favorite cliff in Chu Lai after getting engaged.
Bottom Right: Hugging on their favorite cliff in Chu Lai, 45 years later.

If you'd like to watch an award-winning short documentary film featuring Mike and Shirley on their trip back to Vietnam where they face their pasts and find healing, you can visit www.peacetogetherbook.com and view the film for free.

After the writing of this book, with the help of photos, the kindness of strangers, and the global reach of facebook, we were able to track down Ching Chong. He survived! The orphans of the Van Coi orphanage faced many unimaginable obstacles and many did not survive after the war ended. Ching Chong made it to safety, was adopted by a family in Nha' Trang, and is now married with children of his own. His name is Nhật.

THANKS

I don't know how to fully explain what writing this book has meant to me, how it has changed my life and all of the development I have undergone as a person because of this project. This work has been so wholly rewarding, and I could not be more grateful to have been involved in the creation of this book. To have had time to think, to consider life, people, actions, reactions . . . it's a gift that I can never repay to the one who gave it to me.

That would be God. To try to claim credit for this story, for the ability to articulate it, or even for the circumstances that put me in a position to stay home and focus on this project, would be blasphemous. Just as God has redeemed Mike and Shirley's lives for himself, shown his power through their struggles and triumphs, and written an incredible story with their years, I know he is doing the same with me. To God be the glory of this book. Without him as my guiding light throughout the project, I know I wouldn't have made it.

Writing this book was hard. It required daily discipline and research and interviews and documentaries and books and transcribing recordings and travel and maybe even some writing talent . . . It was hard. But at a certain point, I figured out that I didn't have to feel all the pressure of making it successful. I just had to do my part, to show up and put in the hours, to put my fingers on the keys and tell a story I didn't write. I made a simple deal with God. I will write the words, he will make them good. This way of working allowed me to relax, it allowed me to focus on the story and it protected me from crippling thoughts about my own insecurities as an inexperienced writer. I no longer felt that I had to rely on myself to make this story good. I could shoot for the stars with this project and whether I reached them or not wasn't up to me. How freeing!

The next person who deserves so much thanks from me is my husband, Heath. He heard me dreaming out loud about one day becoming a professional writer. For years I fantasized about having a book with my name on the cover sitting on our bookshelf. As I decided to end my career as a school teacher, he encouraged me to take the leap to stay home, to write my book. In fact, I think he put it like this, "I am not going to let you watch your life pass by without fulfilling this dream. You are going to write a book. Might as well do it now."

I love my husband. At the time, he had no idea that I wanted to write about his parents. And neither did I! He has never been anything but supportive. He supported me in every possible way through this project . . . mentally, emotionally, technologically, financially. Whatever I needed, he was there, all in, with lots of enthusiasm. I

THANKS

remember one day he came home to find me curled up on the couch hiding under a blanket. I told him that I couldn't do it anymore. I was a nobody in the world of writing, and I was foolish to think that I could pull this off. I felt like running away.

Being the wonderful best friend that he is, he sat me up, gave me a stern look and told me that I am Terah Hensley. That I could do anything and that I would finish this book and it would be good. He reminded me that I love writing, that I'm good at writing, and that I needed to keep trying. It was just the pep talk I needed. So were the ones he gave me every couple of weeks for the remainder of this project, and I can honestly say that without his support, this book with my name on the cover, would not exist.

How do I even begin to say thank you to Mike and Shirley? I don't think there are any words I could string together that would give justice to the gratitude I feel. This book wasn't something they wanted. They didn't ask me to write their story down and they were pretty hesitant in the beginning. On the other side of this project, knowing all the history we had to revisit, I understand that hesitation more now than I possibly could have then. They knew that saying yes to me was giving someone else permission to invade their privacy. Their current privacy, their past privacy, nothing would be off limits. And even though I would consider them to be very private people, they chose to say yes anyway.

Over the years, they let me all the way in. It was as if I had been given a set of keys to each of their mental file rooms. The back rooms of their minds where all of their darkest memories were stored and where those memories were supposed to die, to be forgotten and pushed down where they couldn't cause any more pain. It was incredibly risky for them, but with courage and with trust I hadn't yet earned, they gave me those keys.

With them, I embarked on a search and rescue mission for their pasts because I didn't want the world to lose those memories. I didn't think those file rooms should be left locked, primary source war history, archived away in a place where no one else could access it. I believed that bringing back their suffering could offer healing to the world and to themselves. I preached this message to them, and I know I put them through a lot of pain to recover these stories. They believed in the mission too and they were fearless in going back. I watched them remember things they hadn't thought about for decades and I watched it make them old and then new at the same time. Remembering is living art and it's beautiful to watch. How can I ever thank them for this gift?

I owe many thanks to Mike's brother, Terry, for inviting me into his home, letting me badger him with questions about his childhood, and for sharing his own stories of the Vietnam War with me. His willingness to open up and share his memories, many of which were painful to recall,

THANKS

gave me greater perspective and allowed me to tell this story with more accuracy. As for gaining more insight into the life of young Shirley Harbers, I would like to thank her sweet friend Pat, who spoke with me about Shirley's journey of coming to faith in Jesus Christ. She generously offered up her memories of Shirley and the time they spent together serving in the Army, and in the Vietnam War. I would also like to thank Pat and Terry both for their service to our country and for their sacrifice. I hope this book honors the memories they shared and feels true to their own experiences of the war.

Finally, I need to thank my mom. Right in the middle of writing this book, I became a mother myself to two precious little boys. The book had to be put on the back burner for quite some time as I learned my new role in life. When I was ready to get back to writing (several years later), my mom was there to watch the boys whenever I needed her to so that I could finish this work. She was one of my first readers of the rough manuscript and gushed about how good it was, the way moms do when their children create something. She has been an outspoken fan of my projects and my dreams since I quit teaching, and she has supported my efforts all along the way. What a blessing it's been to have her steadfast support over all these years it's taken me to finish this. Thanks, Mom!

BIBLIOGRAPHY

Bell, Kelly. "Deadly Sapper Attack on Fire Support Base Mary Ann During the Vietnam War." HistoryNet. HistoryNet, July 6, 2016.
https://www.historynet.com/deadly-sapper-attack-on-fire-support-base-mary-ann-during-the-vietnam-war.htm.

Butterfield, Fox. "Orphans of Vietnam: One Last Agonizing Issue." The New York Times. The New York Times, April 13, 1975.
https://www.nytimes.com/1975/04/13/archives/orphans-of-vietnam-one-last-agonizing-issue.html.

Clark, Johnnie M. Guns Up. New York, NY: Presidio Press, 2002.

Downs, Frederick. The Killing Zone: My Life in the Vietnam War. New York, NY: W.W. Norton & Co., 2007.

Ellis, Elaina, Lade, Diane. "DEATH'S MESSENGERS." Sun, October 5, 2018. https://www.sun-sentinel.com/news/fl-xpm-1991-02-04-9101060877-story.html.

History.com Editors. "Kent State Shooting." History.com. A&E Television Networks, September 8, 2017. https://www.history.com/topics/vietnam-war/kent-state-shooting.

Klimek, Chris. "More Than Just a Helicopter, the 'Huey' Became a Symbol of the Vietnam War." Air & Space Magazine, February 2021. https://www.airspacemag.com/airspacemag/bell-uh-1h-iroquois-180976722/.

Mazzoleni, Nicoletta, Catusi, Massimo. "The Cuban Hijackings: Their Significance and Impact Sixty Years On." Transport Security International Magazine, October 18, 2019. https://www.tsi-mag.com/the-cuban-hijackings-their-significance-and-impact-sixty-years-on/

ABOUT THE AUTHOR

Terah Hensley is an award-winning documentary filmmaker and a writer of screen dramas and narrative nonfiction. She has a Master of Fine Arts degree in creative writing and a Bachelor of Science degree in Elementary Education. During her years as a public school teacher, she realized that her true passion is in getting to share great stories with others. She left her beloved teaching position to pursue full-time writing with the hopes of capturing life-changing stories to share with the world, both on the page and on the screen. She lives in Winter Park, Florida with her husband, Heath, and their three children, Solomon, Elijah, and Anna Kay. Together, they travel the world collecting memories, artifacts, a few bruises here and there, and best of all, great stories.

www.ingramcontent.com/pod-product-compliance
Lightning Source LLC
Chambersburg PA
CBHW030147100526
44592CB00009B/155